THE JOURNALIST
A Holocaust Story

Oxana Koval Lapchuk
& Valentyn Koval

SUNBURY PRESS
Mechanicsburg, PA USA

Published by Sunbury Press, Inc.
Mechanicsburg, Pennsylvania

www.sunburypress.com

Copyright © 2019 by Oxana Koval Lapchuk.
Cover Copyright © 2019 by Sunbury Press, Inc.

For information about special discounts for bulk purchases, please contact Sunbury Press Orders Dept. at (855) 338-8359 or orders@sunburypress.com.

To request one of our authors for speaking engagements or book signings, please contact Sunbury Press Publicity Dept. at publicity@sunburypress.com.

ISBN: 978-1-62006-159-6 (Trade paperback)

Library of Congress Control Number: 2019951435

FIRST SUNBURY PRESS EDITION: October 2019

Product of the United States of America
0 1 1 2 3 5 8 13 21 34 55

Set in Bookman Old Style
Designed by Crystal Devine
Cover by Terry Kennedy and Monica Nagy
Edited by Lawrence Knorr

Continue the Enlightenment!

This book is dedicated to
the memory of my father, a true freedom-fighter
who was a selfless, committed, and courageous man
that was passionate about his purpose which
never abated even until his death.

TO BE FREE – "Can one truly comprehend
the value of this feeling or state of being
if one has not experienced the opposite?
No. I think not because its value becomes
more priceless to those who know what it
means to exist without it."

—Anatoli, the Journalist

Contents

Preface

This is a riveting account of one man's struggle to survive amid overwhelming odds. The total dehumanization of the individual, the constant fight against apathy and the unceasing gnawing pangs of hunger which assailed the individual in the concentration camp.

However, it was not just about surviving the concentration camps, but the courage to escape from the boxcar when he was literally being transported to his death and the days of wandering in the forest, dodging German soldiers. Where did his strength come from when he was weak from hunger, weighing only eighty pounds? It came from within. His spirit was strong and he fed it with thoughts of living and not dying. He was passionate about this purpose in life and wanted to live to accomplish it.

What causes some to sink into the pit of despair and give up, whereas others would forge ahead despite their circumstances? This is the story of such a man, my father, who, although incarcerated for three years in four different concentration camps, survived. It is told in the first person and is taken from his journals and personal accounts.[1]

The principles he practiced eventually allowed him to triumph and not give in to despair. There are many people out there who are facing challenging situations and they need to have hope to believe that as they practice these principles they too will be able to triumph and overcome. For truly the human spirit is indomitable and can overcome even the weakness of the body to the point where the body must submit to the human spirit. The result: hope that eventually produces victory over our circumstances.

---

1. Some of his personal experiences are taken from a book he published in 1948 in Germany. It is called *We Are Ukrainians* and it was published in the Ukrainian language.

CHAPTER 1

The Arrest

The telephone rang. I stretched out my hand and took the handle. "Hello. This is the editorial office." I heard a sharp voice on the other end say, "Who is this?"

I answered, "The editor, what do you want?"

There was a pause and I could hear in hushed tones a conversation in the German language. I instinctively felt that there was a microphone near the handle.

"Hello, are you listening?" a raspy voice answered after a few minutes.

"Yes . . . I am listening."

"We are calling from the SS. Today at 3 o'clock we want you to come to our office and report to Mr. Schmidt. Do you understand?"

I tried to regain my composure and answered that I would. The clock on the wall showed that it was 2 o'clock now. My thoughts began to swarm within me in a dizzying frenzy. Should I go home first to warn my wife and be prepared to say my goodbyes since I may not see her again? I closed the desk drawers and went into the other office. I called for my co-worker, Mr. Mykolenko and went inside the corridor. Mykolenko swiftly walked towards me.

"I am being summoned to the Gestapo. Apparently, they have been following me. If I don't return by 4 o'clock, please go to my wife and tell her where she can find me."

"Good-bye Anatoli," said the agitated Mykolenko.

I left the editorial office and stepped onto a high porch and began to look around. On the other side of the street in the small square, I saw a man sitting on a bench. No other people were visible. I noticed that it was very cold outside and it was beginning to snow. Can sitting on a bench in the town square bring any pleasure to anyone in this kind of weather? He must be a spy.

I buttoned up my coat, lifted my coat collar and stepped onto the pavement. I hesitated for a moment. Should I go home? I sneaked a glance at the man in the square. The suspicious looking man got up and left. There is no doubt that they have been spying on me. I decided to go home so I could leave my money and documents.

The clock in the city tower showed that it was 2:30 P.M. I decided to take the street opposite the clock tower and walked on the pavement to my house. Our housekeeper opened the door and I asked if my wife, Valentina, was at home (she was a dentist) and where my children were? She answered that my wife was not home yet and my children were asleep.

I went into my office and emptied all the contents of my pockets. I only took some cigarettes, some matches and the key to my front door. I grabbed a pencil and was thinking of writing a note to my wife. What a pity that she wasn't home.

I went into the bedroom to look after my children. My son and daughter were sleeping peacefully, and I covered them with a warmer blanket. I said goodbye in a loud voice, hesitated for a few minutes, then quietly opened the door and went out into the street.

From afar I saw the spy. He quickly lifted his head and pretended that he was looking at the cross on top of the church. I thought to myself, What an idiot. He doesn't even know how to follow me without being detected. I am literally giving myself up to the enemy and will be at their mercy.

Suddenly I remembered that I did not leave my watch at home. I stopped and took off my watch, put it in my pocket and went back to the house. I knocked at the kitchen window and our housekeeper opened the window. I gave her the watch and said, "Nusia, please give this watch to my wife." I headed in the direction of the SS office.

I hesitantly approached the door where I was to report to the SS investigator Mr. Schmidt. I was getting ready to knock on the door when it suddenly opened. At that moment the interpreter, who was a local German named Oscar, stepped over the threshold. I recognized this sadist because he had interrogated me several months ago. He pulled his shoulders back when he saw me and I noticed the smirk on his face when he looked straight into my eyes. I returned his gaze and noticed his black coarse hair underneath his cap which he took off as he closed the door to the other room.

My first inclination was to hit him, but I had to control my urge to do so since I was already in a dire situation. The Gestapo officer, Mr. Schmidt, was sitting at a table, and as he leaned back on the chair he stretched out his legs. He put both of his hands on the table and started banging on the table with his fingers. He had a ruddy, intelligent and swarthy face with thick black eyebrows and he gazed at me with this accusatory expression. I gazed back at him and did not look away. It felt as if an eternity had passed.

"Please sit down," said Mr. Schmidt, motioning to a stool that was by the table. I took advantage of Mr. Schmidt's inattentiveness when I got closer to the table to see if any of my articles were there. But I couldn't recognize anything since all the papers were in a pile. I had a glimmer of hope that maybe they had not gotten their hands on any of my articles.

There was a heavy oppressive silence. The interpreter was looking at a portrait of Hitler which hung on the wall above Mr. Schmidt's head. I sat on the stool as if on pins and needles. The beating of my heart was so loud that I thought they all heard it. I need to get control of my nerves, I thought as I glanced at the papers lying on the table. I began to convince myself that my articles were not among that pile of papers.

The investigator slowly went toward the window near the table and picked up a thin folder. I felt as if lightning had pierced my head because there they were. There was no doubt that this folder contained my articles which they had intercepted. I felt as if a hammer was hitting my heart, and I broke out into a cold sweat.

The investigator stood up, opened the folder and stretched out his arm to give it to me. I tried to restrain my nervousness as I took the folder and saw my article and my signature. As the interpreter was speaking to me in Russian the words of the investigator, I felt as if they came from far away.

"Read it in case you may have forgotten to write something else."

It seemed as if the lines of the article merged together in front of my eyes.

There is no escape, everything is clear to me now. So what comes next: execution?

I had given this article three months ago to the leader of the Ukrainian underground movement, Organization of Ukrainian Nationalists (OUN), after my first release from the Gestapo. A few days before my first arrest, they found my articles in the custody of the leader and three members of the underground. I started to re-read my article with much trepidation.

The biggest enemies of the Ukrainian liberation movement are the local Germans who interpret for the SS. They behave worse than dogs towards the people. If it wasn't for these local Germans, the Third Reich would be clueless. In four months in my city of Kherson, they have shot 120 Ukrainians, 25 were hung and 150 were sent to concentration camps. I do not have the statistics for the other nationalities that were also executed. They execute the prisoners from Friday to Saturday around 3 A.M. in the morning in the ravine near the city jail. They are also taken to the concentration camps every Tuesday. It was dated June 10, 1942.

I finished reading and set my gaze on my signature at the end of the article. They know everything. The investigator took the folder from my hand, and the interpreter broke the silence by his raspy voice.

"Did you assume because it was not written in German we would not be able to read it? Everything you have written in this article has been translated into German."

The investigator jumped on the table and demanded to know to whom else were these articles directed. The Americans? I was astonished at his conclusion. The Americans had never even entered my mind.

The investigator sat down and laid the papers on the table. "Do you know what awaits you?" he screeched at me, and I could feel the spit from his mouth splashing in my direction.

"Execution by shooting," I answered.

The SS officer Mr. Schmidt quickly typed a document and handed it to the interpreter. The document was short and in the text, it read, "The information in this article was written by me and was also intended to be read by the OUN (Organization of Ukrainian Nationalists). For this, I could even be executed."

"Sign it," said the interpreter as he forced the pen into my hand. I signed it.

I could even be shot—the thought swirled around in my mind as the pen tightened around my fingers while I was signing the document.

"Take him away to the same cell where his friends are so they can say their goodbyes."

They brought me out onto the street that cold, starry December night. Then we went across the other side of the street where they took me to the prison yard of the SS. On the way to the prison, the interpreter with a gleeful expression on his face informed me, "Now you will not be able to escape from us."

In the evening they transferred me to cell number 3: prisoners sentenced to death. I found a place in the lower bunk near the wall. They usually shoot prisoners from Friday to Saturday. Today is Monday which means I only have 5 days to live. I am only 30 years old. Will I not live to see my family and friends again?

My thoughts began to swirl within my head and I was not sure who I was to think of at this moment: my children, my wife, my mother or my friends in the underground movement? There were not a lot of people in the cell. Last Friday they emptied out part of the cell when the prisoners were sent out to be executed. I began to feel a terrible weariness overtake me and almost immediately fell asleep. I felt as if I was dreaming and heard someone calling my name—"Anatoli, Anatoli."

The next morning, I woke up abruptly but remembered that I had a dream about a church with a cross on top of the steeple all lit up. What could this mean? I was not a religious man but wondered if this was a sign that I will live and not be executed.

When I woke up, I noticed the door of the cell was open and I saw the rays of the sun on the floor. There was also a SS officer standing in the middle of the prison cell, yelling at me to go.

Is today the day I am to be shot? Came the fleeting thought.

I went outside and stood for a moment by the prison. It was such a beautiful, warm day that it was hard to believe this was the month of December. Even the sparrows were chirping happily.

"Come now," screamed the policeman as he pushed me. I saw a group of my comrades standing in front of the prison as I approached them. I asked them, "Is this the day we are to be shot?" But no one replied to my query.

Nearby was an SS officer with an automatic rifle and Oscar the interpreter was standing next to him. I also saw the investigator Mr. Schmidt as well and a group of policemen. Suddenly the interpreter Oscar spoke, "You will not be executed, but instead, you will be sent to work in a concentration camp in Nikolajew, Ukraine. How long you will be there depends on how good a worker you are." He then turned to the SS officer and pointed his finger at the automatic rifle. "There are thirty-four bullets in here, so you need to obey their commands; otherwise, you will be shot."

We were then led through the streets of the city. I carefully looked at all the people to see if my wife was among them or any of my friends. There was no one that I recognized except on the corner of one of the streets I saw my friend Alex. As we got closer to where he stood, he slightly nodded his head in recognition. Stay well my friend, I thought to myself.

As they were taking us to the railway station, the SS officer with the automatic rifle approached me and said, "We are not the KGB. We will not execute you since you did not come against the Germans actively but only in your writings."

We got to the platform of the train and noticed that it was overcrowded with soldiers going on leave back to Germany. On the carriage was an inscription, "Only Germans allowed here." We were shoved into the back section of the train. A German soldier seemed to take an interest in us and asked the Gestapo officer who we were. He answered, "Ukrainian Nationalist bandits."

He seemed delighted with the answer and sat down. The Gestapo officer settled down near the window, put his rifle on the seat next to him, took a document from his briefcase and started to read it. The rays of the sun shone through the window, and since the paper was thin, you could actually see what was written. I bent down as if to tie my shoelaces and read a sentence but could not understand it all since it was written in German:

> ". . . The leaders of the Ukrainian organization
> in the city of Kherson for an undetermined time
> are being transferred . . ."

The Gestapo officer then stood up and folded the document. The train chugged on past tranquil fields and sleepy towns. Outside the train windows, people were going about their daily work, oblivious to the fate of the "Ukrainian bandits," whose lives were about to change forever.

On December 24th, 1942, the gates of the concentration camp "Vodokachka" closed behind us as we were herded in like animals.

CHAPTER 2

Background

My father, Anatoli Tryschewskij, alias Valentyn Koval was born in the city of Kherson, Ukraine in 1912 to a family of intellectuals and freedom fighters. His mother Eugenia, was supposedly a Ukrainian Jew from Zurich, Switzerland, although it was never proven that she was Jewish. She married his father Peter who was from Ukraine. He also had a younger sister and an older brother. Kherson was a large urban center in southern Ukraine and was situated on the right bank of the Dnieper River. It had a large Jewish population and many of them worked in the factories and owned businesses as well.

During his early years, he went to public school and eventually finished high school. His family would always gather together to discuss the political situation during that period which revolved around the repressive policies of the Soviet regime.[1] His father and mother were both teachers and many of this aunts and uncles were also

---

1. Stalin had orchestrated a man-made famine called Holodomor (murder by starvation) between 1932–33 where over seven million Ukrainians died. Many others were executed or sent to labor camps because they wanted to break free from the Communists and establish their own independent state.

Anatoli at 27 years old as production manager in
a huge factory in 1939, Kherson, Ukraine

teachers and writers. He discovered his love for writing at an early age and eventually decided that at some point he would be a journalist.

He continued his formal education and for the next three years studied tractor technology and engine building in an industrial institute. Upon completion, he trained to be a pilot and received his wings. Eager for

Anatoli and his wife, Valentina, in 1939

employment, he got himself a position as a production manager in a huge factory which manufactured engines for tractors. The plant had roughly 30,000 employees, with 10,000 having to report to him daily.

During this period of his life, he met his wife, Valentina who was studying to be a dentist. They had two children, a boy and a girl and when his wife eventually got her degree they were able to afford a housekeeper. Unfortunately, World War II broke out, and my father established himself as a leader of the

Ukrainian underground movement. He quickly took control of the underground newspaper and became its editor. Everyone involved in the movement fought furiously against the Russians and the Germans for the independence of the Ukrainian state.

This led to his arrest by the Gestapo in December of 1942, as depicted in the previous chapter. He was deported to a concentration camp in Nikolajew, Ukraine called "Vodokachka," which means Water duck in English. It was about forty-four miles from his home town of Kherson. Unfortunately, the city of Kherson, which was the town he was residing in with his wife and children, suffered great devastation and many lives were lost there during World War II. The next chapter will cover his experiences in the concentration camps.

CHAPTER 3

The Concentration Camp Years

VODOKACHKA

I started my new life in the concentration camp Vodokachka in Nikolajew, Ukraine on December 24, 1942. I will not dwell on my experiences in this camp except to say that I did not know at the time that I would be a slave for the next two and a half years.

We had to work very long hours and were given a diet that barely sustained our power to work. The production quotas were so high that it was beyond the strength of many of the prisoners. Fortunately, we could correspond with our families and receive parcels. I would not have survived if it had not been for my wife who would frequently send me parcels of food. At this camp, which was more like a labor camp, we were allowed visitors from our immediate family.

My wife, Valentina, visited me a few times, but it was not an easy journey. It was winter time and sometimes she had to walk because buses did not always operate due to the inclement weather. The camp was seventy-one kilometers from where we lived in the city of Kherson.

Many of my comrades from the underground movement were interned with me so we did manage to have a lot of comradery and discussions, even though they worked us so hard. Despite that, it gave us the will to carry on and to have hope for our eventual release. Unfortunately, we labored there for over nine months and then they deported most of us to the concentration camp Buchenwald in Germany near the city of Weimar.

"LITTLE CAMP" AT BUCHENWALD

I arrived there on October 5, 1943, with a transport from Nikolajew together with 604 other deportees.

I was registered as a political Russian (since Ukraine was not yet recognized as an independent county), and as you can tell by the names on the list most of us were either Poles, Ukrainians, Russians or other Slavic nationalities.

I was in complete shock when I arrived there with the other prisoners. As we entered through the gate there was an inscription, "Each to His Own," (translated from the German) which could only be read from the inside. I saw the crematorium to the right which had a high, thin chimney and rows of barracks which housed the prisoners. We were taken to the quarantine area, which was called the "Little Camp," separated from the main camp with barbed wire.

They shaved off our hair, gave us those striped concentration camp uniforms and assigned each of us numbers that they affixed to the left side of our shirts. My number was 25362 and I was assigned to live in block or barrack number sixty-three. Once we completed our four-week quarantine period we would be deported to

No.	Nr.	Name	Vorname	Geb.	Ort	Beruf
531.	25537	Tolkatschew	Wiktor	29. 6.24	Cherson	Monteur
532.	705	Trebuch	Dmitro	5. 3.16	Dubowij Poselok	Tischler
533.	353	Tregubow	Andrej	7. 8.96	Jelanez	Agronom
534.	404	Tribrat	Filip	10.10.00	Baschtanka	Landarb.
535.	447	Tribrat	Timofij	12. 7.09	Baschtanka	"
536.	362	Trischewskij	Anatolij	14. 5.12	Cherson	Ingenieur
537.	601	Tschablenko	Pawlo	23. 6.23	Gorodok	Schlosser
538.	613	Tschebotarjow	Arkadij	3. 3.02	Konstantinowka	Landarb.
539.	306	Tschekanzow	Kuzma	25.12.05	Sucho-Jelanez	Schmied
540.	337	Tschelowan	Stepan	25. 8.03	Ganowka	Schlosser
541.	652	Tscherewik	Wasilij	10. 8.20	Burowka	Install./Zimmerm.
542.	334	Tscherkassenko	Grigorij	25. 5.03	Kazanka	Mechaniker
543.	504	Tscherkes	Michail	29.12.25	Nikolajew	Schiffsbauer
544.	377	Tschernega	Jakiw	10.10.14	Nikolajew	Landarb.
545.	397	Tscherwonnyj	Dmitro	1. 4.04	Subbotzi	Schuhmacher
546.	612	Tschumatschenko	Iwan	6. 1.08	Marijanowka	Automech,
547.	373	Tschuprina	Awram	17. 2.92	Sergejewka	Landarb.
548.	476	Tulejkow	Anton	11. 1.00	Nikolajew	Schuhmach.
549.	596	Twerdij	Dimitrij	21. 7.00	Krasnopolje	Landarb.
550.	260	Turtschak	Iwan	5. 1.94	Majerowka	Traktorf.
551.	581	Tyschtschenko	Wasilij	19. 3.02	Bereznegowatoje	Schmied
552.	341	Ulezko	Nikolaj	10.11.14	Rossosch	Kraftf./Schloss.
553.	464	Warenik	Kondrat	9. 3.25	Michajlowka	Landarb.
554.	653	Warfolomejew	Nikolaj	17. 2.20	Iskrino	Schlosser
555.	327	Wartschenko	Petro	25. 6.14	Nowo-Nikolajewka II,	Landarb.
556.	501	Wasilenko	Andrej	11. 8.11	Orel	Elektriker
557.	134	Wasilinenko	Iwan	23. 6.12	Werschino Kajanka	Traktorf.
558.	635	Wdowitschenko	Jakow	1.11.21	Nadeshdowka	Landarb.
559.	634	Wdowitschenko	Petro	12. 9.13	Nadeshdowka	Schmied
560.	354	Wdowitschenko	Fedir	19. 9.10	Michajliwka	Schriftleiter
561.	571	Wischenskij	Radion	23.11.16	Koluzke	Traktorf.
562.	595	Wizenko	Semen	15. 3.09	Cherson	Landarb.
563.	336	Wlasenko	Dmitro	17. 3.07	Bolschaja Alexandrowka	Ldarb.
564.	275	Wolkow	Fedor	8. 2.05	Roxandrowka	Landarb.
565.	559	Wolobojew	Maxim	30. 8.01	Wladimirowka	"
566.	481	Woloschin	Petr	25. 6.10	Nowo-Odessa	Schloss./Kessels...
567.	370	Wolyk	Nikolaj	5. 5.22	Aul	Schlosser
568.	361	Worobjew	Leonid	21. 8.08	Sewastopol	Zimmermann
569.	553	Worona	Michail	10. 1.80	Nowgorodka	Eisenbahner
570.	326	Worotinzew	Iwan	23. 9.00	Nowyj Bug	Landarb.
571.	295	Woskresenskij	Alexandr	9. 6.11	Krasnowidowo	Arzt
572.	329	Wowka	Sawwa	23. 4.85	Pogreby	Koch/Korbmacher
573.	600	Wowtschenko	Wasyl	10.12.25	Krupoderensi	Landarb.
574.	190	Wosnesenskij	Petro	30. 5.24	Jejsk	Maler
575.	297	Wyschenskij	Wasyl	13. 9.18	Kaluga	Landarb.
576.	614	Wysotschanski	Grigorij	18.12.01	Sadowa	Landarb.
577.	409	Zabloskij	Wladimir	17. 7.24	Kazanka	Kraftf.
578.	381	Zachartschenko	Konstantin	29.4.12	Nowo-Dmitrowka	Techniker
579.	564	Zabeglowskij	Leonid	20. 1.29	Nikolajew	Schuhmacherlehrl.
580.	247	Zagrbelnyj	Wasilij	14.12.22	Wosnesensk	Autoschloss.
581.	296	Zajtschenko	Iwan	5. 5.02	Nowo-Grigorowka	Landarb.
582.	568	Zajsow	Petr	15. 4.00	Jawkino	Schuhmacher
583.	444	Zaliwadnyj	Wiktor	15. 9.21	Nikolajew	Maschinensetzer
584.	621	Zaporoshtschenko	Iwan	26. 5.15	Sofijewka	Fischer
585.	550	Zarikowskij	Iwan	17. 9.25	Baschtanka	Schlosser
586.	459	Zawalko	Alexandr	26.12.24	Suworowka	Kunstmaler
587.	554	Zazulinskij	Jakow	16.12.10	Odessa	Ingenieru
588.	458	Zelenskij	Filipp	8. 1.04	Wysche-Tarasowka	Schuhmacher
589.	701	Zelin	Andrej	5.10.95	Wodjano-Lorena	Landarb.
590.	546	Zelin	Iwan	17. 2.04	Zaretschje	Schlosser

This is page 10 of an eleven-page transport document of 604 deportees from Nikolajew, Ukraine, to Buchenwald. They are listed as Russian Civil Workers. My father is #536. To the left of his name is his assigned prisoner number (25362). To the right is his date of birth, town, and profession (engineer). (Courtesy of Transportliste Außenlager Schönebeck 20.10.1943, Buchenwald, 1.1.51/ITS Digital Archive, Bad Arolsen)

KL: Hollerith erfaßt   Häftl.-Nr.:

Häftlings-Personal-Karte

Fam.-Name: T r i s c h e w s k i j   Überstellt   Personen-Beschreibung:

Vorname: Anatolij   am: an KL.   Grösse: 174   cm

Geb. am: 14.5.12 in: Cherson   Gestalt: schlank

Stand: verh.   Kinder: 2   am: an KL.   Gesicht: oval

Wohnort: Cherson,   Augen: grau

Strasse: Ul. Strokata 14   am: an KL.   Nase: gerade

Religion: orth. Staatsang.: UdSSR   Mund: gew.

Wohnort d. Angehörigen: Ehefrau: am: an KL.   Ohren: norm.

, Walentina T.   Zähne: vollst.

W.O.   am: an KL.   Haare: blond

Eingewiesen am: 5.10.43   Sprache: russ. ukr.

durch: Sipo Nikolajew   am: an KL.

in KL.: Buchenwald   Bes. Kennzeichen:

Grund: Russ. Zivilarbeiter   Entlassung:

Vorstrafen: am: durch KL.:   Charakt.-Eigenschaften:

mit Verfügung v.:

Sicherheit b. Einsatz:

Strafen im Lager:

Grund: Art: Bemerkung:

I.T.S. FOTO No 0 5975   Körperliche Verfassung:

KL./5/4.43 - 500000   11513/Ne

My father's Prisoner Personal Card that was issued by the Gestapo upon arrival at the camp. All personal information is listed: name, date of birth, relatives, weight, build, etc. (Courtesy Anatolij Trischewskij, Buchenwald, 1.1.5.3/7296620 bis 7296626/ITS Digital Archive, Bad Arolsen)

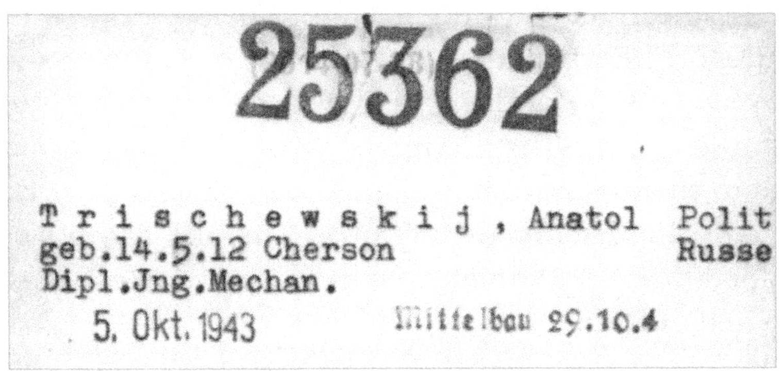

My father's prisoner number assigned to him in Buchenwald – 25362. He is listed as a Politcal Russian. (Although he was Ukrainian, at that time Ukraine was still under soviet rule.) His profession is listed as Graduate Engineer, Mechanic. (Courtesy Anatolij Trischewskij, Buchenwald, 1.1.5.3/7296620 bis 7296626/ ITS Digital Archive, Bad Arolsen)

different sub-camps as forced laborers to help build the V-1 and V-2 rockets for the Germans.

The Little Camp was on the north side of the camp and consisted of twelve army horse stables which they used as barracks. There were six compartments on each side that were set up so three prisoners could sleep on top of the other divided by a beam. In total there were seventy-two platforms and it was so cramped that it was impossible to turn or change sides.

The conditions here were much worse than in the main camp and its inmates were subjected to the greatest suffering. There were no windows, no running water, and virtually no heat in the stables. There was only one latrine and many prisoners had to use their food bowls as latrines at night. Drinking water was also very scarce and the food rations were much smaller than what the inmates received in the main camp.

Daily life here was very monotonous and exhausting. They would wake up us between 4 and 5 A.M. for roll call and keep us standing for hours before they sent us off to work. Fortunately, my time here was very short, a little over three weeks which was probably the reason for my survival. The Germans would then send many of us to the different sub-camps to work as forced slave labor in the armament industry. The one camp we all dreaded being sent to was Dora or as it was referred to "the hell of Dora."

We heard that the living and working conditions at Dora were horrific and most that were sent there died within weeks or several months. They had to sleep and work in these underground tunnels which were damp and cold. It was almost impossible to sleep there because of the constant noise of the machines and the thick dust in the air that made it difficult to breathe. Unfortunately, a lot of my comrades were transferred there, but I was transferred to the sub-camp Julius Schönebeck on October 29, 1943. I was considered a skilled laborer because of my background and experience so I assume that is why they sent me there and not Dora.

JULIUS SCHÖNEBECK

The sub-camp Schönebeck was a small camp which provided labor to the Junkers Aircraft and Engine Company. The SS offered slave labor to factories for payment and selected those inmates who would be considered skilled laborers, such as myself. Most of the prisoners were from Russia, Ukraine, Poland, France, Belgium, and the Netherlands. There were frequent transports to this camp from Buchenwald and other camps such as Dachau.

We had to work in twelve-hour shifts and usually, our day began at 4:30 A.M. I had the task of manufacturing electrical parts for the V-2 rockets. Several times a day we had to endure long roll calls standing outside in the cold with clothing that did not keep us warm. The food was barely enough to keep you alive and eventually you would starve to death. We slept in unheated wooden barracks and had one thin cover to keep us warm. Most of the camps had watchtowers and this one was no exception. It had two watchtowers and high barbed-wire mesh fencing about three meters high.

In addition to all this suffering and exhaustion, we were beaten and mistreated by the guards and the Kapos. The Russians, Ukrainians, Jews, and gypsies were particularly subject to abuse and humiliation from the SS because we were considered to be sub-human.

- 2 -

51	Polit. R.	25630	Panarin, Michail	18. 5.25
52	Pole	22492	Parul, Ludwig	26. 7.2o
53	Polit. R.	26462	Patapow, Wladimir	16. 2.21
54	Polit. R.	2667o	Pazew, Wladimir	24.12.18
55	Polit. T.	22507	Peck, Karel	1o. 5.o4
56	Polit. R.	2646o	Popow, Alexej	14. 7.21
57	Polit. R.	26495	Popow, Nikolaj	15.1o.13
58	Polit. R.	26664	Rudj, Georgij	2o. 9.12
59	Polit. R.	24715	Samojlow, Konstantin	14. 4 .25
6o	Polit. R.	26661	Semikras, Grigorij	6.11.18
61	Polit. R.	25133	Sinij, Wiktor	11. 8.24
62	Polit. R.	253o4	Sinjakin, Dmitrij	18.1o.18
63	Pole	22498	Skoropad, Mikolaj	12. 5.25
64	Polit. R.	26464	Skatschkow, Anatolij	15. 4 .2o
65	Polit. R.	25657	Slastuchin, Alexandr	16. 3.13
66	Polit. R.	24777	Slotin, Wladimir	11. 2.o4
67	Polit. R.	26674	Smirnow, Iwan	6. 4.99
68	Polit. R.	24668	Suschtschenko, Wiktor	5. 9.25
69	Polit. R.	25478	Susdalew, Michail	2o.1o.o4
7o	Polit. R.	25389	Stamat, Mifodij	11. 5.99
71	Polit. R.	26463	Tarschikow, Petr	1. 6.23
72	Polit. R.	26488	Temoschenko, Genadij	15. 3.16
73	Polit. R.	25362	Trischewskij, Anatol	14. 5.12
74	Polit. R.	247o1	Truchin, Nikolaj	9. 5.99
75	Polit. R.	24612	Winogradow, Pawel	23. 3.18
76	Polit. R.	2537o	Wolik, Nikolaj	5. 5.22
77	Polit. R.	25481	Woloschin, Petro	25. 6.1o
78	Polit. R.	26457	Zajzew, Petr	23. 7.2o
79	Polit. R.	25546	Zelin, Iwan	17. 2.o4
8o	Polit. R.	25449	Zmijewskij, Boris	12. 3.25
67	Polit. R.	24687	Wlasenko, Jakow	24. 1.21

Page 2 of a transport document to the sub-camp Julius Schönebeck. My father is #73. He is listed as a Political Russian. Included is his prisoner number and date of birth. (Courtesy of Transportliste Außenlager Schönebeck 20.10.1943, Buchenwald, 1.1.51/ITS Digital Archive, Bad Arolsen)

The constant pangs of hunger and the long hours of labor led to extreme exhaustion. I realized that in order not to lose hope altogether you had to strengthen your human spirit by speaking to it so that your body would submit to your mind. So I kept visualizing myself as a free man and refused to give in to despair and hopelessness. This was not easy since none of us had any idea how long we would be here and when, if ever, we would be liberated.

However, many of us found comfort by forging strong ties with those of our own nationality and me especially with the political prisoners who shared the same passion as I did for freedom and independence. I spent a year laboring in this camp before I was transferred again to another sub-camp on October 23, 1944, named "Heinrich" near Rottleberode.

ROTTLEBERODE

Initially, Rottleberode had been constructed as a sub-camp of Buchenwald, but on October 28, 1944 the former sub-camp of Buchenwald became an independent concentration camp of the Mittlebau/Dora complex. Some of the sub-camps of Buchenwald administratively became sub-camps of Dora. Therefore, the prisoners imprisoned in these sub-camps, in administrative terms changed from prisoners of Buchenwald to prisoners of Dora. You will notice on the document on page 22 that I was officially registered as a prisoner in the administration of Dora and no longer of Buchenwald.

About sixty of us prisoners, mostly Russian, Ukrainian, Polish, and French were transferred to Rottleberode from Schönebeck. There were about 1000 prisoners here and that number would increase to 2000 by April 1945, right before we were evacuated. This sub-camp was established so that German aircraft components could be assembled underground. The aircraft factory at Schönebeck was authorized to convert the Heimkehle caves into an underground facility.

We were housed in a three-story building which had been a porcelain factory. It was outside the village of Rottleberode and not far from the railway station. Our sleeping quarters were on the first and second floors and the building was surrounded by watchtowers and an electrified fence. There were a kitchen, washrooms, and a storeroom on the ground floor. There was also a

Once the sub-camp of Rottleberode became an independent camp of Mittlebau/Dora, some of the prisoners of Buchenwald became prisoners of Dora. Above is my father's personal card showing the administrative change. (Courtesy Anatolij Trischewskij, Buchenwald, 1.1.5.3/7296620 bis 7296626/ITS Digital Archive, Bad Arolsen)

courtyard between the building and the electrified fence which was used as the roll call area.

Life here took on the same monotonous rhythm as the other camps. They would wake us up at 3:30 A.M. and then after we washed, we would have to stand outside in the courtyard for roll call. Unfortunately, we had to march three kilometers every day to the caves where we worked. Once we arrived at the entrance of the tunnel, we were re-counted and went to our respective workplaces in the underground tunnel factory. We got a twenty-minute break around noon so we could eat the small amount of food they provided but it was a starvation diet, hardly enough to sustain a grown man.

O·U·,den 23.1o .1944

A u f s t e l l u n g
der vom Kommando Julius nach Kdo.Thyra überstellten Häftlinge:

Lfd. Nr.	Haftl.Nr.		Name	Vorname	Geb.Dt.	Beruf	Facharb.
1.	477	R	Samojlow	Nikolaj	7. 2.24	Dreher	ja
2.	1723	R	Dgestow	Michail	2o. 6.11	Fräser	ja
3.	3352	R	Teslenko	Igor	8.o3.18	Fräser	ja
4.	342o	R	Kowal	Nikolaj	1o.1o.25	Fräser	ja
5.	5221	P	Nowicki	Jan	24.1o.19	Dreher	ja
6.	79o8	R	Karpez	Iwan	18. 9.23	Hobler	ja
7.	8991	R	Sienkiewicz	Nikolaj	27.11.22	Reinigung	nein
8.	9169	P	Czopek	Stanislaw	8. 1.22	Dreher/schlosser	ja
9.	1182o	P	Dlugokecki	Stanislaw	4.11.21	Drher	ja
1o.	12698	R	Schabetinskij	Pawel	1. 8.23	Fräser/dreher	ja
11.	14334	N	Hermann	Joseph	17.12.19	Hilfsarb.	nein
12.	14691	R	Schewerda	Wasilij	19. 1.11	Reinigung	nein
13.	14783	P	Sider	Mieczyslaw	15. 1.23	Dreher	ja
14.	15o15	R	Kondraschow	Boris	17. 7.25	Dreher	ja
15.	15o35	R	Mortschinowskij	Wikter	18.12.13	Fräser	ja
16.	15179	P	Mirka	Waclaw	2o. 4.22	Dreher	ja
17.	15199	R	Ponomarjew	Iwan	16. 9.24	Bohrer	ja
18.	1525o	R	Awramenko	Wiktor	27. 4.2o	Schlosser	ja
19.	15252	R	Fedtschenko	Sergej	25. 2.21	Fräser	ja
2o.	15479	R	Krytschun	Wladimir	4. 3.2o	Fräser	ja
21.	15514	R	Lukaschewitsch	Petr	18. 6.11	Dreher	ja
22.	15559	R	Kalnizkij	Stefan	24.12.2o	Dreher	ja
23.	15613	R	Breshnow	Jegor	1o. 4.o8	Fräser	ja
24.	16832	T	Kubik	Karl	14.11.13	Fräser	ja
25.	17oo1	T	Sip	Jan	3. 8.19	Fräser	ja
26.	17oo6	T	Kouba	Frantisek	13. 1.18	Werkz.schleifer	nein
27.	17281	T	Steinbach	Josef	11. 7.13	" "	nein
28.	2o837	F	Leturneaux	Vikter	18.11.22	Prüfer	nein
29.	23o27	R	Tyndyk	Wasilij	1o. 8.13	Bohrer	nein
3o.	25362	R	Trischewskij	Anatol	14. 5.12	Dreher	ja
31.	29211	P	Tarka	Wladyslaw	12. 5.18	Schleifer	ja
32.	29218	P	Tomkiewicz	Stanislaw	25.1o.99	Härter	ja
33.	3114o	F	Jouniaux	Ernest	1o. 7.o1	Ma.-Schlosser	ja
34.	33236	P	Bobrowski	Tadeusz	11.12.23	Dreher	ja
35.	35865	R	Osiptschuk	Wladimir	18. 2.2o	Fräser	ja
36.	37265	R	Podsolkin	Leonid	29. 1.25	Dreher	ja
37.	3834o	F	Poncet	Roger	11. 3.17	Prüfer	nein
38.	38812	F	Michellon	Felix	7. 5.96	Spritzer	nein
39.	41432	P	Proch	Eugeniusz	17. 9.21	Härter/Schle.	ja
4o.	41454	P	Bucyk	Wasyl	12. 3.12	Fräser	ja
41.	42893	F	Pinaguy	Maurice	11. 5.22	Prüfer	nein
42.	43493	F	Coteret	Andre	14.1o.13	Fräser	ja
43.	5o9o2	R	Schurtin	Alexej	5. 8.19	Schmied/Schlo.	nein
44.	51299	F	Isvelin	Rene	1o.1o.2o	Werkz.Schleif.	nein
45.	51427	F	Cottet-Emard	Rene	5. 2.15	" "	nein
46.	51428	F	Carre	Andre	7. 6.o4	Fräser	ja
47.	52394	F	Bourdelat	Jean	16. 4.22	Gewehr-Rapat	nein
48.	53389	F	Maillet	Delphin	22.11.25	Drher	nein
49.	53633	R	Petrusenko	Iwan	6. 9.25	Werkz.Schleif.	nein
5o.	62103	R	Furmanow	Alexej	12. 3.2o	" "	nein
51.	62656	P	Zajko	Eduard	1. 2.21	Härter/schm.	nein

Page 1 of a two-page transport document of sixty prisoners from Schönebeck to Rottleberode. My father is #30. His occupation is listed as a skilled lathe operator. (Courtesy of Transportliste Außenlager Schönebeck 20.10.1943, Buchenwald, 1.1.51/ITS Digital Archive, Bad Arolsen)

After we finished working there was another roll call and we were marched back to the camp.

I was given the duty of operating a lathe twelve hours a day in this dark, underground dungeon about one hundred meters in depth. At the time I only weighed eighty pounds and was already hatching a plan to escape from this wretched inferno. There was a man, a Kuban Cossack, who worked next to me as a milling machine operator. I approached him with the idea of planning an escape and he seemed to be interested but did not take much initiative to discuss it further. So, as in the past, I had to depend on myself and my wits to figure out a way to escape.

Then in late November 1944, Erhard Brauny was assigned as the new camp commandant of Rottleberode. He mistreated the prisoners and beat them daily with clubs, sticks, or whips. He also kicked inmates and when drunk would shoot at the prisoners every night. I took the brunt of many of his beatings and he was particularly brutal towards the Russian and Ukrainian prisoners. However, the Jewish prisoners suffered the most and he beat them frequently with rubber hoses and clubs. He would also cut the rations of the Jewish prisoners and go into anti-Semitic rages along with his Kapo, Walter Ulbricht. They were both hated among the prisoners and were responsible for causing the deaths of many of the inmates.

However, in early April 1945, the SS decided to evacuate all the camps because the US troops were advancing towards the Harz Mountains. An order was given that no living inmate was to be allowed to fall into the hands of the enemy.

The Escape

A hundred kilometers from the concentration camp Rottleberode was a military battle raging between the German and the American armies. The leaders of the camp were preparing us for evacuation. On the evening of April 5, 1945, on the side of the highway by Rottleberode by the city of Nordhausen, columns of prisoners stretched around the highway surrounded by the police and their dogs.

We were divided into hundreds. I was in the last section of the column with my friend, Victor. Those who did not have the strength to move or were too ill were left behind in the concentration camp.

"They will undoubtedly be destroyed," remarked my friend Victor who was walking beside me.

I tightly squeezed his hand and said, "Well Victor, this is our last chance to save our lives. There will be no other chance to escape."

The sky was hidden by rain clouds, and it started to sprinkle. From far away, you could hear gunshots. You could hear American planes. The highway goes past the village of Stampeda, where just yesterday we were building aircraft in the underground factory next to the rocky hills.

Where are they taking us and what will they do with us? This was foremost in the mind of all the prisoners.

In front of the column, we heard the rumble of cars. The column of marching prisoners had to stop abruptly. As it turned out, the road was destroyed by bombs from the airplanes flying overhead, and the cars of the German troops were stuck in the deep holes. We had to take a detour. When we passed the bombarded area, they stopped one hundred of the prisoners in one of the columns and divided them into groups of fifty. Victor and I happened to be in this group.

Finally, I thought I may have the opportunity to realize my three-year longing to escape. The SS officer who was assigned to our group told us, "We are going to pull our cars from the pits and if any of you attempt to escape, we will shoot you."

The surrounding area was so dark, it was as if you had on blindfolds. The police and the military had to use flashlights to be able to see. Then they separated us into groups of ten, and for every group of ten, they assigned five policemen with dogs to guard us.

As I looked to the sky in the south near the city of Nordhausen, I noticed that it burned with a red glow. I gladly looked at the glare of the huge fire in the distance. "That is what they deserve," said Victor loudly as he came up to me. He was waiting for a sign from me when to escape.

I heard freedom, freedom as if someone was whispering those words in my ear. I was very agitated, and my heart was beating rapidly. Only two steps into the darkness, two steps and . . . then!

On the right, the sound of gunfire resounded. A human solitary cry was mingled with the barking of the dogs. Then we heard this brutal shout from the darkness, "Get in line, get in line, get in line!"

We started to hurry, and the officer was shouting as he held a flashlight behind us.

"One tried to escape, but he made a mistake because our dogs are smarter than you. Now he is dying in the bottom of the pit. If any of you dare to escape you will get the same treatment."

My hopes were dashed. Is it impossible to escape? I began to persuade myself that it was possible. However, you had to plan it carefully and wisely. I just noticed that Victor was not beside me and called out to him, "Victor, Victor!" But there was no answer. Maybe he got frightened. The night passed, and it was getting light again. I could feel the warm spring rain on my face and a thick fog covered the ground.

My longing to escape had not materialized so far. I stood above a deep hole that was made by a bomb and was holding one hand over the side of the car trailer. At the bottom of the pit, a prisoner that had been torn apart by the dogs was dying. He also had probably longed to escape.

"What a senseless way to die," I said with a loud voice.

"That is the same fate that awaits us," said Victor who came up from behind unexpectedly.

I flinched at the sound of his voice, and from that moment, I began to loathe him. I turned around and gritted my teeth: "I do not want to see you anymore. After tonight our friendship is ended."

Victor did not pay attention to my words and as he looked around said, "How can we escape when we haven't eaten for several days? We are barely able to stand on our feet. The Americans are very near. Let's wait for them, and they will free us."

"You will be waiting for a German bullet and not freedom," I answered angrily, and I walked away from him.

It was now day. We were hungry and wet mud clung to our bodies as we were pulling the car trailers that collapsed into the craters during the night. Suddenly we heard sirens coming from the surrounding cities and villages and the announcement of an air raid. The policemen became enraged and generously beat us with rods but some of them helped us to pull the car trailers. Finally, we got them out of the pit, and without any rest, we headed for the highway. I heard the shooting coming from the airplanes and you could hear the sound from the airplanes more clearly as they got closer.

How long will my strength hold out?

The policemen kept inflicting us with blows on our backs with long whips as they hurried us along the highway. The whips made a whistling sound as they cut through the air and cut into our backs with a burning sensation of pain. Every time I heard it whistle over me I would squint from the pain when it struck my back.

If they would only aim at my head, maybe it wouldn't hurt as much. After every strike, I would bite my lips, and they would start to bleed. The tears would flow from my eyes, and I would get angry with myself for being so sensitive. It seemed to me that the others did not feel the pain of the blows on their backs as I did.

The corpses of the prisoners who were shot lay on both sides of the road. They probably tried to escape during the night and were caught. The highway was strewn with scattered hats, berets, and blankets. Many of the prisoners tried to lighten their loads so it would be easier to walk.

Near the town of Hartzungen along our path, we passed through a concentration camp which was divided into two halves. When the trailer came alongside the camp we squeezed closer during our march. There was no one left at the camp since everyone had been evacuated several days ago. The windows and doors of the barracks were open and on the field a pile of corpses was visible.

"Move quickly, move quickly," said the SS officer as he growled at us. The painful burning blows that were inflicted on us caused us to walk faster. Ahead of us, some papers were picked up by the wind. They flew up in the air as if they were butterflies and then they fell on the asphalt. I recognized that these papers were banknotes of different denominations—five, ten, fifty, and one hundred rubles.

The sound of the whip interrupted my thoughts and the Frenchman who was marching on the right of me screamed, raised his hands and fell on the asphalt. The policeman took out his pistol, shot him and left him behind.

Through the hustle and bustle, you could hear the clattering of the rubber tires of the trailer. Ahead of us was the city of Niedersachswerfen. We quickly ran across the main street and stopped by the railroad station. We left the car trailer.

As they led us to the train we saw the bodies of the prisoners on the platform. They were shot because they had tried to escape during the evening transport. Just as they loaded us into the open boxcars, we heard the sirens go off. Overhead we saw the American fighter planes. The policemen surrounded the transport and bowed lower towards the ground. The commandant, Erhard Brauny of the concentration camp, Rottleberode where I was an inmate, happened to position himself in the same cable car on the opposite side of where I was seated. As the American fighter planes again appeared in the sky the prisoners squeezed closer to each other and waited. I had a great desire to see a bomb tear into pieces the concentration camp commander who sat opposite me. I did not even consider my own safety.

The last plane disappeared behind the mountain leaving a trail of smoke. Puffing heavily, the train left the station. It arrived at a small station called Osterhagen, and then they unhooked the box car which did not move for several hours.

Where are they taking us? The prisoners questioned among themselves.

Today they gave us no food or water. In the evening it started to rain and on the floorboard of our car, which had no roof, were puddles of water. I covered myself with a blanket and stood on top of the board to study the surrounding area. To the north of the station, about three kilometers was a thick forest. This was the beginning of the Hartz Mountain foothills. I focused my gaze on the trees, which were high and very thick.

Now a person can hide behind those trees. Over there one can be free.

In the meantime, along the train on both sides, a sentry was posted—SS officers with their dogs.

How can I escape?

My brain began to work overtime under the pressure. An argument ensued in the car between the Poles and the Ukrainians. I couldn't contain myself any longer, so I turned around and yelled at them. "You idiots. Today or tomorrow may be the final days of our lives, so why should we argue when we have so little time left?"

The arguing ceased. A policeman was assigned to guard each car since it was evening. Unfortunately, the policeman that was assigned to our car sat right next to me on a small stool that he had brought with him. He appeared to be about forty years old and of average height. As he inspected the living dead and fearing for his own safety, he put his rifle against the wall next to him. After that, he put his hands on his knees and closed his eyes.

I glanced at him and thought: What are his hopes and dreams?

As I continued to glance in his direction, I noticed he had a ring on his middle left finger. I was horrified because I noticed he had the emblem of a skull and crossbones on his ring: a symbol of death! I immediately turned away.

No. This is not possible. I want to live. I must live. I will live.

I will live!! I kept repeating this over and over in my mind. Death was not an option. Not when I was only thirty-three years old and had a lot to accomplish yet in my life.

The rain did not stop. I pulled the blanket over me and sat against the wall of the cable car. The water from the rain created small puddles on the floor of the train as it splashed on the sleeping prisoners. Somewhere in the distance, you can hear the sirens from time to time. You could also see flashing red sparks as they exploded in the sky.

I could not close my eyes the whole night since I kept thinking about escaping . . .

The sky seemed to turn grey and it continued to rain. And today they did not give us anything to eat. It was already the third day without food or water. Will my strength hold out?

I found several prisoners on the train who agreed to escape with me. We all talked over the best way to do this. If the policeman who was guarding us did not fall asleep, we would kill him.

In the evening, the wind quieted down and it stopped raining. The moon began to emerge from behind the clouds. I thought to myself, Oh my God, what is this? Send a storm and send downpours, I pleaded.

It was already dark and the policeman who had not changed his position from the previous night started to doze on and off. All those who had decided to escape went to the opposite side of the cattle car where the policeman sat. By midnight he had fallen asleep.

The silence was deafening. Even the slightest noise sounded like a clanging symbol. Our hearts were beating so loudly we were afraid it would wake up the policeman. Our fate will now be determined at this moment–life or death.

We quietly unlocked the door of the car, lowered ourselves and one by one we crawled underneath them. I was the fifteenth prisoner to escape. I laid underneath the car and noticed there were other cars on the neighboring tracks. I cannot recall how I managed to crawl underneath four of the cars and cross over a wooden fence near that station. All I can remember is that I found myself in a field.

As I turned to the left I saw my comrades running towards the forest whereas I ran in the opposite direction. The wet heavy clay clung to my shoes and started pulling me towards the ground. At that moment I heard gunfire and the barking of the dogs as the guards pursued the prisoners.

Without stopping I pulled out a small bag from my pocket that contained some ground black pepper. My hands were trembling as I sprinkled it behind me because I knew the dogs would not be able to detect my scent and I kept running further.

I finally found myself in the forest. It seemed dark, thick and mystical to me since I did not understand it nor was I familiar with it since I grew up in the city. But at this moment it was precious to me. I fell on my knees near a pine tree, grabbed the trunk of the tree and kissed it as I wept profusely like a small child. It seemed as if the forest began to speak these words to me, Freedom, freedom, freedom!!

All of a sudden, I heard a groan nearby. My first thought was, could this be a dog? I jumped to my feet, grabbed a knife from my pocket and leaned against the pine tree. The groaning continued. As I listened intently I breathed a sigh of relief since I realized it was a person and not an animal.

"Who are you?" I asked in the dark. His voice sounded constrained as he answered me, "I am Polish. My name is Pawel." Then a figure rose up from the ground. I recognized this man who escaped from the cattle car ahead of me. We hugged one another and were grateful that we had survived the worse so far.

Now we need to go quickly towards the hills and into the thickest part of the forest. As we ran deeper and deeper into the forest, the prickly branches tore our clothes and cut our faces and arms but we ignored it and kept running.

We stopped at a large field and since it was a very starry night I started looking for the North Star to find the direction north which I spotted near the Big Dipper.

"Do you know how to navigate by the stars?" I asked Pawel. He replied he did not know how to follow the stars so then I asked him. "Do you want to be rescued by the Americans, the English or the Russians?"

"It's all the same to me. I really don't care," he replied.

"Well it matters to me," I said. "I have determined to go to the Americans and if you decide to come with me we can go together. If not, then let us part now and go our separate ways."

"I will go with you to the Americans," he said.

So once again I looked up at the North Star and with faith in the belief that I could use it as a road map proceeded in a northerly direction. We walked towards our destiny . . . freedom.

CHAPTER 5

Despair

We proceeded to walk through the forest as the dry branches crackled underneath our feet. We walked very cautiously straining our ears to hear even the slightest suspicious sound. At any moment you can stumble across an army of German soldiers.

An air raid was about to ensue since we heard sirens coming from behind the forest. I walked ahead and Pawel followed behind me. I would stop and listen intently from time to time. Pawel seemed indifferent to his fate or mine and his passivity led me to despair several times.

Whenever I would stop suddenly because I thought I heard a noise, he would keep walking instead of helping me to detect what kind of sound it was. Other times he would lag far behind me and even disappear into the darkness of the forest. Many times, I waited for him to catch up and even had to turn back several times to look for him.

Twilight was approaching very quickly and every moment counted. It became clear to me that I had to rely on my own wits not only to save myself but him as well.

You can easily lose your way in the forest if you cannot see the northern star to go in a northerly direction. Therefore, every time I would see a clearing in the forest I would look for the northern star to lead me in the right direction even if it meant going deeper into the forest.

However, the first night since our escape we were very fortunate. The sky was clear and the sound of the sirens pointed us in the direction of a densely populated area close by, probably a city or village. It was dangerous for us to remain in the forest during the daylight hours.

As my thoughts began to swirl within me, I heard a shrieking sound above my head. I stopped dead in my tracks and broke out in a cold sweat. It was a large bird that flew from one of the branches of the tree where it was perched.

"What is that?" cried Pawel in alarm. I breathed a sigh of relief and moved from my stationary position. We could see in front of us between the trees that it was starting to get light. Daylight was approaching. As we went to the edge and looked around we saw that the forest had ended.

Before us, in the early haze, we could see rows and rows of plowed fields. Behind the fields, there was a small hill and then we saw the forest begin again after the hill. There was no doubt in my mind that the people in the surrounding cities and villages had been informed about our escape.

"We have to quickly and imperceptibly run across the field to that forest behind the hill," I spoke to Pawel as I waved my hand in that direction. It was completely light by now and we had not even gone half the distance. We had wet mud splattered all over our bodies from all the days of walking and running. Pawel was far behind me and probably had no strength to proceed further.

We were in a dire situation. At any moment we could be discovered by the Germans. I could clearly see the bell tower of the village church from my left which was only two kilometers from me. Then I heard the dogs barking. At that moment I felt as if the nervous tension in my body had reached its limit. I was completely drenched in sweat and felt my temperature rising.

My only thought was to keep moving forward. Finally, I made it to the forest. I hid behind the trees that were nearest to me and then I turned around to see if I could get a glimpse of Pawel. He was still far away and you could see his concentration camp uniform. I looked around to see if anyone was following us but did not see anyone.

As Pawel was approaching the forest, I ran ahead, grabbed his arm and pulled him into the forest. We rested for a few minutes and continued ahead. "We need to hide somewhere in the thicket and stay there until the evening," I said but then stopped abruptly to observe our surroundings.

It seemed as if the light from the forest shone in every direction. We saw trees planted in rows near a village. However, the trees were small and not planted that close to one another. It was obvious that we would not be able to hide here.

We could not waste any time but had to make every minute count. I saw some bushes very close by where we could hide. We ran towards the bushes and realized we had to disguise ourselves since our uniforms were visible.

I took a knife out of my pocket and asked Pawel, "Do you have a knife?"

He answered, "Yes I have."

I then used my knife to cut out a thick branch from the bushes and Pawel followed my example. "They will not take me alive," I told Pawel. "We do not have the right to sleep lest they catch us unawares."

We sat in the bushes with our backs against one another. Each of us had the responsibility of observing the village from our vantage point. I had never in my life desired anything as much as I did at this moment, to see thick, high green grass instantly grow all around us to shield us from being discovered by the Germans.

I started to fall asleep. Do not fall asleep. Do not fall asleep. I felt as if an electric current went through my body and I immediately woke up. Pawel in the meantime had leaned forward and fallen asleep. I got angry and thought to myself, why is he sleeping? Without getting up, I hit him on the head with my branch. Pawel leaped to his feet in a frightened manner as he blinked his eyes.

"Sit and don't sleep," I ordered him. "We could be caught like blind cats if we do not stay alert. We do not have the right to sleep." Pawel sat down quietly. The hands of the clock on the church tower struck midnight.

Oh God, it seems as if we have sat by these bushes for an eternity and there seems to be no end to this day. Then I heard dogs barking and children's laughter in the direction of the village.

"Lie down," I whispered to Pawel as I fell to the ground. The children and the dogs came very close to the bushes where we hid. Then we carefully got up and went to the edge of the forest that was opposite the village. I looked all around the surrounding area and breathed a sigh of relief. There was a forest in front of me with high mountains.

My nerves started to calm down but the pangs of hunger began to overtake me. To climb uphill without any food to strengthen me is tantamount to starving to death. I glanced at Pawel as he stood helplessly beside me with his head downcast. It seemed as if he had lost all hope and had fallen into despair about his fate.

"We should be able to find some food in this village, otherwise we will perish," I said aloud.

"I will not steal any food," answered Pawel resolutely.

I looked at him in amazement. "What do you mean that you will not go?" I questioned him. "This is the first time in my life that I have met anyone like you. Has fate punished me to be bound to you during this struggle for our life?" I reacted with anger.

"Tomorrow the Americans should be here so why take such a risk?" said Pawel.

"And what if the Americans do not come tomorrow?" I questioned him.

"Then we have to surrender to the Germans." He answered. When he spoke those words, I felt as if my heart had turned to stone.

"Do you realize what you are saying?" I asked visibly shaken by his words. "If we give ourselves up to the Germans they will hang us or shoot us." Pawel held his tongue and kept silent.

It has now become very dark. As I looked up at the sky, I found the northern star and without saying a word, proceeded north towards the mountains. I tried not to think about the conversation with Pawel. There was a battle going on within me not to give in to despair especially when I was involved in a struggle for the preservation of my life. I was afraid of losing hope. At this moment I felt that Pawel's despondency and lack of faith could also affect me adversely. He was becoming a heavy burden to me and I did not want to fall into disbelief and despair.

As we continued to walk you could feel the rustling of the leaves underneath your feet. I felt certain as we got closer to the village they would have a covered pile of potatoes or beets that they kept in the winter months in a small pile. I decided to look for it and would frequently squat to look over the land to see if I noticed a small mound sticking up from the ground.

My desire came to pass. I noticed the silhouette of a mound in one area and flung myself on top of it. It was a small pile but what did it contain? I dug up the ground and grabbed a beet which I ate after I cleaned off the dirt. It was very bitter.

Then we heard the sirens. We quickly grabbed the remaining beets and left the area. The sky lit up and it almost appeared as if the darkness was dispelled because of the intensity of the red flames from the blasts. The ground shook violently because of the impact of the explosions but then everything became quiet.

We went in the direction of the mountains and came across a river as we tried to climb the steep cliffs. Our attempts were unsuccessful since we would frequently roll down the cliffs as if into oblivion. As we kept moving further to the north the cliffs got higher and the forest thicker. In the morning we found ourselves on a high cliff in a forest with trees that had been cut down. The trees were chopped close to the ground and you could see all the stumps sticking out. When it got lighter we noticed at the foot of the slope was a highway where German troops were moving to and fro.

Suddenly over our heads, we heard the neighing of horses and cars screeching. I lifted my head upwards and froze. There was another highway about thirty meters from us. The German army was also trudging on this highway. The danger was so obvious that I immediately fell to the ground and wrapped my feet around the short stump and told Pawel to wrap his feet around my shoulder.

The mountains were high and you could see the snow in some places. My flesh was almost numb from crawling on the cold and frozen ground. Above the mountains, you can hear the roaring of the planes. The soldiers were retreating and started running to the mountains in our direction grabbing the stumps of the trees. The airplanes noticed the movement of the troops and fired at them with their machine guns. You could see the bullets whizzing through the air all around us and the impact caused the stones on the ground to be lifted into the air as well.

Pawel started praying. The fighter planes flew away but then the bomber planes took their place. They dropped bombs on the upper and lower part of the highway and then flew away. It was completely dark by the time we could lift ourselves up from the ground. Our bodies were so cold that we could not even feel any warmth inside of them.

It seemed too dangerous to go deeper into the mountains. The frost and the dimming of our hope that the

Americans would arrive any time soon forced us to change our course of direction. I decided to continue north since I felt the Americans would come from that direction and the northern star in the sky would guide me. We went down the slope and it seemed as if there were blinking lights up ahead. I stopped momentarily and assumed that these were fireflies and went straight towards them.

"Halt, halt!" A few meters from us we heard those words and then the sound of machine guns. As the bullets whistled over our heads, I fell on the ground, then I jumped to my feet and bolted to the left. When I felt that the danger had passed, I stopped. It was quiet all around me except for the rustling of the leaves on the trees.

So much for the fireflies, I thought as I spit on the ground in anger. What happened to Pawel? I sat on a rock and listened intently. "Pawel," I said quietly.

"Where are you?" he answered. We were together again. After a short walk, the mountains ended and the forest began to thin out. We would be taking a risk if we went any farther since we could not hide anymore in the forest. We need to go in the other direction. We went over a mound and descended downwards.

"There is either a river or a swamp ahead of us," I remarked as I turned around to look at Pawel. We eventually came to a lake and walked along the shore. It seemed as if we walked for a long time but there appeared to be no end to the lake. I became upset because instead of going north we were going to the west but that was the direction the lake took us.

Then ahead of us in the darkness, we stumbled upon a few small houses. We climbed over the fence, cut across a garden and found ourselves on a wide street in a small town. Our shoes clattered so loudly on the pavement that it alerted the dogs and they started to howl.

We quickly ran across the street and climbed over another fence. Again, we found ourselves in a garden. We went across the garden but were too weak to climb over the wire fence. Then we overturned several pillars to free ourselves from being stuck in this garden so that we would not be taken captive. We were in a desperate situation and became discouraged when we found ourselves back at the shore of the lake.

As the morning was approaching we saw a small forest not far from us which we entered. It was the third day since our escape and we had finished eating the beets that we had dug up from the ground. I reminded Pawel that we needed to look for some food in the German village.

He turned pale and quickly answered me. "We need to surrender to the Germans, the Americans are nowhere in sight, otherwise we will die of hunger." This is the second time he has spoken like this.

I became very anxious but managed to take control of myself and said. "So you want to surrender? Don't even think of doing this right now because I will also be captured. When it is dark, you can go wherever you want even if I have to remain alone but I will never surrender."

I was under tremendous pressure all day since I had to keep an eye on Pawel. I also kept my knife and stick by my side so I would be alert and ready for any confrontation with the Germans. We sat with our backs to one another and I thought if Pawel rises to his feet

I will have to decide what to do. However, Pawel never moved—he was fast asleep.

It became dark and the stars were shining brightly in the sky. I got up and went into the forest and did not say a word to Pawel. However, he followed me. I began to breathe easier since the lake ended and now we were headed towards a field. The ground had been recently plowed and the dirt was loose. I squatted several times to see if I could dig out some seeds to eat.

Up ahead I saw some small wooden buildings and realized these were all greenhouses. As we approached one of the greenhouses I unhooked the latch and went inside. I then lifted the window frame and felt the ground with my hand. Nothing seemed to grow there except for some grass. I tore off a stalk and swallowed it. It tasted like kohlrabi but how can my hunger be satisfied with this kind of food?

I lifted several other window frames but everywhere it was the same. Out of anger, I decided to open all the doors to the greenhouses. The morning frost will take care of the rest. Pawel also quietly opened all the doors to the greenhouses. We broke through the garden fence and left the area continuing to go north.

My thoughts began to trouble me because I did not know where we could hide during the day. I began to search for a forest, no matter how small as we continued moving forward. I noticed in front of us an area that seemed very dark so I walked in that direction. We were very fortunate because as it began to get light, we found a small area that had several thick trees planted in rows.

I was so relieved that I lay down on the dry leaves. My nerves were stretched like the strings on a violin and

I kept hearing buzzing sounds in my head. Suddenly I heard voices nearby and the sound of boots clattering. I jumped to my feet, walked to the edge of the trees and lay down again. There was a highway right next to the forest and I could see the movement of the German infantry. To my amazement, I heard two soldiers near the very edge of the forest speaking in Russian. One of them said, "Where are they taking us since the Americans are only twenty-five kilometers from here."

I almost shouted for joy. After the soldiers passed by, I found Pawel and told him what I had heard. The German troops were retreating and the Americans were coming. Pawel was overjoyed and promised me that never again will he talk about surrendering.

However, my joy was short-lived because I was consumed with an overwhelming desire for water. I found a birch tree among the trees and I knew that in the spring it yielded sap. I began to cut sections of the trunk of the tree but it yielded no sap.

Now with the hope of a quick rescue from the Americans, we stayed in the forest until night. Then when the stars appeared in the sky we continued our journey. We crossed over a field and came upon a seeder which we knew contained grain. Our joy had no limits. We lifted the lid of the seeder and found an abundance of oats. I grabbed a mouthful and kept eating to my heart's content. When we cleaned out the whole seeder we continued our trek.

In front of us was a village. We moved very carefully and Pawel was several steps behind me. We came upon a highway. I fell to the ground and in the deep furrow pushed myself along the path. Suddenly, my hand touched someone. I leaned back and froze. Something moved in the deep furrow and I heard someone snoring. I carefully moved to the left and again I stumbled upon another human being. I moved to the right and the same thing happened.

These were tired, retreating German soldiers who were sleeping in this forest. I crawled back to the deep furrow and started moving backward. Suddenly a few steps from me I heard the voice of a frightened German soldier. "Halt." The rays from the flashlight showed the figure of my friend, Pawel. Without being conscious of what I was doing, I leaped to my feet and ran to the left. Several shots were fired from the revolver and you could hear the cry of my friend mingled with the cries and panicked shouts of the Germans.

After several minutes I listened intently towards the direction where my friend Pawel was killed. Now I am alone and I must continue walking to the west. I could hear the sound of artillery very near. The bullets were hissing as they flew over my head. After each shot that was fired, I saw flares coming from the guns. They were shooting from west to east. But who? Was it the Germans, the Russians, or the Americans?

CHAPTER 6

At Last Freedom

It started to drizzle and the cold wind penetrated my skin through my concentration camp uniform. I am standing in the middle of a field and am troubled as I observe my surroundings. There are no trees and no place for me to hide. Now they will be able to see me. Is there no salvation for me? What should I do? What should I do?

My nerves were on edge and I didn't even feel the pangs of hunger any more or the extreme exhaustion that has plagued me all these months. Dark and bright spots were floating in front of my eyes. What should I do, what should I do?

The sky began to clear up and in the morning mist, I saw a mound with a few trees in front of me. I need to go in that direction as fast as I can so I mustered all the strength I had and ran. My legs were not cooperating with me and I had to use my hands to lift them because the wet mud was sticking to my shoes.

Finally, I got to the mound and found myself in a recently plowed field. I climbed over several of the furrows and dropped to the ground. My head was spinning and my eyelids were drooping from lack of sleep. I scraped off some of the chunks of clay and then I lay in a ditch which had been dug deeply by a giant plow.

As I lay there with wide open eyes I looked up at the sky. What has caused me to survive the horrific circumstances of my life in the last several years? Was it the will to live and the desire to accomplish specific goals in my life? What was the motivating force that caused me to carry on when others seemingly gave up and lost hope? Can the spirit of a man overcome even the weakness of the body to the point where the body must submit to the spirit? Sometimes it seemed as if death was inevitable. The sparkle of life may fade in one's body and yet somehow, suddenly a flame of life ignites it again.

It began to rain again and next to me was a puddle of water. The ground was cold and my body was getting numb. I could catch the droplets of rain with my parched lips but then I began to feel feverish. As I was sifting through my thoughts, I was reminded of what was said to me many years ago. It was said that there will come a time in your life when you will suffer hunger and cold. And here I am laying in the water on the cold ground. I could die today or tomorrow laying in this muddy ground or maybe the Germans will capture me and hang me. And how I want to live. I scolded myself for thinking such thoughts and dismissed them.

It was around midday; the sky had cleared up and the sun was shining. I looked up at the sky and above me was a lark fluttering its wings. He was warbling and I thought how long has it been since I saw you on the steppes of Ukraine. I am not alone because you are with me. My soul began to feel joyful and light.

I felt a strange silence all around me. Now and then a squadron of silver bomber planes flew close to the ground. I realized that I had not heard sirens since morning. I wondered why the planes were flying so close to the ground. What can this mean? I lifted myself up very carefully using my elbows and looked around. I could see the whole area from my hiding place. There was a town on my right only several kilometers from me. I saw tall factory buildings with chimneys but had no idea what kind of town it was or its name.

I continued to look around and saw an endless stream of cars on the highway. Then to my left, I heard an airplane and as I looked in that direction the plane was flying straight at me. I fell into the ditch and held my breath. The plane was circling around the small mountain and flying lower and lower. I clearly saw white stars on the wings of the plane but to whom do they belong? Not the Russians since they have red stars and not the Germans since they have the swastikas. It must be the Americans and then deep within me I thought, Freedom, can this truly be the fulfillment of my longing and desire to be free?

Then a strange thing happened, as I was on my knees I did not feel any joy about being rescued. Instead, the thought of eating came to me like a bolt of lightning. I grabbed a half-eaten, leftover beet from the ground and as my hands trembled, I lifted it to my mouth but instead threw it away. Now I will not need to eat beets any more. Then somewhere deep in my heart, rage took hold of me and burned within me. I looked with envy at the town before me and thought, I will get everything I need over there. My head began to make a buzzing sound again so I lay back in the ditch, hoping to get a little rest before I ventured out to the town, only a few kilometers ahead of me.

The sun is coming up and it appears that today will be a sunny day. I tried to stand on my feet but when I did I fell. The earth seemed to disappear underneath my feet and was somewhere far away from me. I stretched out my hands and grabbed at the clumps of dirt and then lifted my stick off the ground. I lifted myself up again and carefully repositioned my feet as I walked towards the town.

Spring has arrived. You could hear the birds chirping and on the left, the grass was starting to shoot up from the ground. I came to a cornfield and as I looked more closely I saw some spinach. I looked away in disgust. It was loathsome to me because of all the years I spent eating spinach in the concentration camps. I went through a small section of the cornfield and came upon a road that should lead me to the town. I saw a pool of water up ahead. I bent down, cupped my hands so I could drink the water. It was dirty and tasted nasty.

I sat down and looked into the water. I was horrified at the reflection that stared back at me. I saw someone with burning red swollen eyes and bristles of hair that jutted out from protruding jaws. Could this really be me? I shuttered and walked faster towards the town. I squeezed the stick in my hand and continued walking. I could not find a living soul anywhere. I finally came to a neighborhood and approached a yard from behind which seemed to be in disarray. I saw broken empty wine bottles, helmets, rifles and gas masks scattered here and there.

I saw a German man with outstretched arms laying under a tree. I picked up a heavy pistol from the ground as I got closer to the dead German. I checked the cartridges in the gun and only one was missing. A few steps from me on the left I saw a cart containing some household goods. Maybe it contained some food. I put the pistol in my pocket, leaned against my stick and ran straight for the cart. Behind me I heard someone say, "Halt, halt."

I stopped and turned around to see who it was. It was an old German woman with a hump who stood about ten steps from me. Behind her was a large hole which must have led to a bomb shelter. I gritted my teeth and approached her. The old woman looked at me for a few minutes, started to scream hysterically and then climbed into the hole. I heard as she shouted, "Prisoner, Prisoner."

"Do you expect me to be in hiding the rest of my life," I shouted as I sat near a hole on a dry tree stump.

No one appeared so I pulled out my revolver and cocked the trigger. I then shouted as loud as I could with all my strength, "I need food, I need food."

After a few minutes, another old woman with disheveled hair and red eyes from lack of sleep climbed out of the shelter and offered me a morsel of bread. I grabbed a scrap of bread with trembling hands and swallowed it whole. Then she said, "There is no market here, there is nothing to eat."

Then a three-year-old boy climbed out of the shelter. He reminded me of my children and I began to feel sorrow about their fate. Where are they? What has happened to them? Will I ever see them again? Amid these thoughts, I waved my stick at the German woman and shouted, "I need food." The three-year-old boy screamed out loud and hid in the shelter, whereas the old woman fell to her knees.

I turned around and left the garden to find a house or a building that was not destroyed. In the courtyard, there were geese, chickens and in the stables, you could hear the pigs grunting and the sound of cows. I got angry at the old German woman since she lied to me about the food.

I decided to go further down the road and came to a house. The doors and windows were destroyed by the blasts from the bombs. I need to find some food and civilian clothes, I reasoned to myself. Just as I was about to lift my foot onto the porch someone pinched me from behind. The pistol flew out of my hand and I fell under the wall. Then two huge dogs appeared and started walking towards me.

The first thought that came to me was that they will tear me to pieces. I broke out into a cold sweat since I was in no condition to fight with anyone. Fortunately, the stick remained in my hands. I was able to get back on my feet as I leaned against the wall. I saw the old German woman whom I first encountered in the court-yard, laughing spitefully at my dilemma. As I tried to pick up my pistol, the dogs started barking and rushing towards me.

You need more courage, no matter how weak you are, I thought to myself. So I lifted the stick and swung at the dogs. Then the most amazing thing happened. The dogs started wagging their tails and took off in the opposite direction. The old German woman could not believe what had just happened and opened her mouth wide in total disbelief. I looked at her, picked up my pistol and calmly stepped out into the street.

CHAPTER 7

A Time of Anger and Revenge

Leaning on my stick for support, I found myself standing on a wide asphalt highway and observed the city before me. The buildings were covered in layers of dust from the smoke caused by the fires. *That is what they deserve.* The buildings were destroyed by aircraft bombers on both sides of the highway. Everything was overturned and scattered like toys made from paper. You could see many feathers spinning round and round as the wind carried them hither and thither.

There were deep chasms in the ground that had been ripped open by bomb blasts. A thick layer of fragments from the bricks and planks covered the highway. There were no Germans in sight. Maybe they are afraid and hiding somewhere. In front of me, to my left, a car drove up to one of the buildings that had survived the blasts. Some people came out of the building and helped the ones that just arrived to unload some boxes. I moved closer to them and sat on a rock.

I immediately recognized that they were Ukrainians because of their conversation and the clothes they wore.

Two of them stopped what they were doing and walked over to me. They looked exhausted and troubled. They both appeared to be about 30 years old.

"Good day," they greeted me.

"Good day," I answered them and touched my parched lips because I was so thirsty. These were the first civilian Ukrainians that I have encountered since I have been free. I wanted to hug them and talk to them. "I want to eat. I need food," were the only words I could blurt out for now.

One of them turned around and ran into the building and the other one sat beside me.

After a short silence, he said to me, "You were in a concentration camp." It was obvious since I still wore the uniform, and answered him in the affirmative.

In the meantime, his friend returned with some bread and a liter of milk in a mug. He gave it to me and spoke these words to me, "Don't eat everything at once because you will get sick."

No way was I going to take his advice. I grabbed the bread and the liter of milk and without taking a breath ate as fast as I could. Some drops of milk dripped down my beard. "Thank you," I said after I finished eating.

"To your health," they spoke in unison.

After a few minutes of silence, one of them asked me for how long I had been free and if I had seen the Americans or the Russians. "Do you think they will come here and are you waiting for them," he asked.

Silence. I was the first one to break the silence. "I don't know who you are and I don't know how far the Russians are from here, but I would advise you not to fall into their hands," I answered. Again, silence and then one of them spoke up. "Do you think it is better if we go to the Americans since they would be fairer than the Russians?"

I told them that is what I intend to do and then asked them, "What is the quickest way to get to the center of the city?"

"Go this way, under the bridge," spoke one of the men as he waved his arm in the right direction. We said our farewells and I went on my way.

I saw a group of young women as I was walking behind the bridge to get to the town. They were carrying packages, clothes, and shoes. One of the women left the group and asked me, "Who are you?"

I answered, "I am Ukrainian." All of a sudden, I found myself surrounded by this group of young women and they offered to give me some sugar but apologized that they did not have anything else to give me.

"Why don't you put some of the sugar in your pistol," advised one of the women as she filled up my pockets.

"Sir, go as quickly as you can to the town and take whatever your heart desires," they all instructed me.

"The Germans have all fled and you can change into the clothes that they left behind," one of them said.

The girls went on their way and I remained on the highway, my pockets full of sugar. I stood there for a long time and watched them as they walked away from me. Tears began to flow from my eyes, but this time they were tears of joy.

As I walked farther, I noticed that the highway merged with the main street of the city of Nordhausen. The houses here did not suffer much damage from the bombs as on the outskirts of the city. Along the street stood American tanks and jeeps. The soldiers treated the people with chocolates, biscuits, canned food, and cigarettes. It seemed as if a thousand hands were stretched out towards them so they could grab something for themselves.

I saw people walking out of the partially destroyed buildings carrying the spoils of war in their hands. I turned into a side street with the hope of finding an unoccupied building. After inspecting a few buildings, I came upon a two-story house. The front door was closed so I went into the yard. A bomb which had fallen between the yard and the building made a deep hole. The deep hole in the meantime had filled up with water. Every window in the house was broken, so I left my stick and crawled into the house through the opening of the broken window. Apparently, I had crawled into the bedroom and you could tell that this dwelling had at one time been occupied. The fragments of glass, clay on the walls and a thick layer of dust on the furniture and bedding pointed to the fact that no one lived here anymore.

I went into the corridor and climbed up to the first floor. The door was open and in the hallway of the study, was a dead man lying face down. I recognized by his uniform that he had been a former concentration camp inmate. I stepped over the corpse and went into the study. The luxurious and expensive furniture, the library, the radio and the large Persian rug on the floor did not attract my attention since I was looking for the kitchen.

I desperately needed to drink something to quench my thirst since I had just eaten a large amount of sugar. I opened the door of the office to another room and was overjoyed at what I saw. There were plates on a table that contained some soup that was half eaten and some moldy, smelly meat in a saucepan. I walked over to the cupboard and opened the door. My eyes could not believe what they saw? Ham, bacon, sugar, wine . . . I was beside myself.

I grabbed the ham and began to eat it. Then I approached the table and pulled out the tablecloth. The plates fell on the floor and broke into fragments making a loud, clattering noise. I removed everything that can be eaten from the cupboard and laid it all out on the table. Then I went into the kitchen and everything seemed to be in its proper place.

Next to the stove was some coal and firewood laying on a tile board and there were special cabinets that contained different kitchen utensils. In the closet by the wall, I found canned fruits and vegetables. It also contained some onions, beets, and potatoes. I took the onions and the beets and placed them on the table in the dining room.

Then suddenly the thought came to me that someone could take all this food from me so I began to worry and did not know what to do. Should I eat now or should I find a way to hide and protect my food? I was tormented with thirst. There was no water in the pipes. I grabbed a pail, tightly closing the door behind me, went out into the yard to get some water from the deep hole created by the bomb. I lowered the pail into the water but could not pull it out. I had no more strength left. So I plunged my face into the water and drank. I tried again to lift the pail with both hands on the bracket, spilling half of the water but managed to carry the rest into the kitchen.

It was starting to get dark outside but I found some candles in the cupboard. I put three of the candles on the table and lit them. Then I lowered the drapes over the windows and began to breathe more easily. I sat by the table and began to eat. I could not figure out what to eat first. But on what will I sleep? Tonight, I will sleep on the floor, I decided. This is the first time in years that I have slept in a house. I leaned on the table and fell asleep.

As I slept all my dreams revolved around food and eating. Wake up and eat, wake up and eat. It was difficult to breathe since it seemed as if someone was choking me. I opened my eyes and became extremely frightened since I felt like my insides were going to burst open. I did not think very long but turned aside and put my fingers in my mouth. I threw up and felt better but regretted wasting all that food. I fell asleep for a few minutes and began to eat again. This process repeated itself about three times until morning. Sleep, eat, and throw up. However, in the next few days, I began to feel like a human being again.

I could shave, take a bath, and dress in the clothes I found in this house. I was amazed at the large selection of women's and men's clothes I found in their wardrobe closet, including linens and shoes. I also found many woolen and cotton materials in their drawers. In one of the drawers, I came across a package of sleeveless satin shirts that had not even been worn yet. This was probably one of the trophies won on the eastern front by the SS officer who owned this apartment. These high-quality silk shirts and linen bedding must have come from foreign textile mills.

However, I did not pay attention to these expensive items because my psyche was still consumed with the fear of hunger. Wherever I went I was tormented with the thought that I did not have enough food and anyone could steal it from me. Instead, I kept taking food without stopping to the dining room and kept this up for a week without even going out into the street. Gastrointestinal issues plagued me every day but I did not pay attention to it since I felt that I was gaining strength in my body.

When I finally went out of the house, I saw the streets of the city filled with the ruins of the multi-level buildings and broken telegraph poles. The electric wires on the burned-out telephone poles were hanging in mid-air and this probably was the military's network of communication. In many places trains, buses and cars were overturned. Even though I had great difficulty getting through all the debris, I got a good view of the city. In several places, I came upon many human corpses covered with rags and you could see arms and legs sticking out of the bricks from some of the other corpses. The human masses flowed continuously into the city and like locusts, they crammed into the surviving factories and buildings. Instantly they filled all the basements and corridors of the buildings that were not destroyed.

Some of these buildings at one time were used to manufacture tobacco. You could hear the crowd yelling and cursing at the Germans. Their rage was directed toward the German perpetrators of this holocaust. In the crowd, you could see the former prisoners of the concentration camps because their uniforms were visible. "We will kill the Germans," shouted the foreign masses of people drunk with freedom and alcohol. Now nothing stood in their way to seek revenge on those who had committed these horrible crimes against humanity.

The center of the city of Nordhausen also suffered damage from the bombs. Many of the buildings had been destroyed and you could see broken furniture, household goods and pieces of broken glass from the windows on the streets. The American soldiers calmly watched the human drama going on in front of them. Many of the soldiers had similar ethnic backgrounds to those who suffered at the hands of the Germans. However, it was noticeable they did not have the same kind of hatred for the Germans since they did not experience their brutality and for many of them, it was their first time in Europe.

There was a group of soldiers however, who stood in front of an overturned train that had been bombed and they would stop those who passed by to check their documents. They would be detained if they were Germans and the soldiers would invite the foreigners to hit them in the face. I stood on the side and as I looked on, it reminded of my life in the concentration camp. They apprehended five Germans and they stood there with their heads bowed. Their loose hair fell over their foreheads as if to hide the bruises on their faces. And I once stood in their place, as I remembered my many years of suffering and abuse in the concentration camps.

Where is your pride? Where is your courage, now? You supermen. I wanted to go up to each of them and spit in their eyes. Should I go up to them and hit them? Should I hit them for all the people they have murdered and tortured for no reason? However, I noticed a group of young men and women bustling around the Germans.

One of the young men approached a group of soldiers and started talking to them while he pointed his finger at one of the Germans. Apparently, he recognized the foreman from one of the factories where he worked. He was a cruel taskmaster. He was abusive to the workers and beat them. He also forced them to work very long hours even beyond their strength.

The soldiers then conferred with one another. One of them found a car that was parked nearby. He sat in the car, started the motor and drove up to the German. The others grabbed the foreman and placed him on top of the radiator. Then the soldier drove the car through the streets of the city. The German firmly grasped his hands around the radiator so he would not fall and was burned. He had an expression of horror and disbelief on his face.

I then mingled with the human masses in the streets since I had no concrete goals or plans. At the corner of a lane, I noticed two women sitting in a cart that was pulled by a horse. One of them held the reins of the horse and yelled at the horse to stop. When the cart straightened out, I approached the women and asked them if they were Ukrainian?

"Yes, we are from Poltava."

"And you?"

I did not know how to answer them so kept silent.

"Why are you standing there, throw us your jacket and sit here with us. We are going to drive back to our camp which is not far from the city. Everything is good there."

I thought, "Maybe it is so." I gave them my jacket and lifted myself up into the cart.

"At first, I thought you were a German," said one of the women.

"I did also," confirmed the other woman. I am sure it was because of the clothes I was wearing which I took from the German home. I did not respond to their query but told them I was only free for the last few days.

"Were you in a concentration camp?" they questioned me. "There are many here like you. Right now, we are driving past them. They are now living in German houses. The Americans evicted the Germans and the former prisoners are now living in their rooms. That is what the Germans deserve," said the woman fervently as her face turned red.

We left the city and to the left of the highway was a row of buildings. American medical workers (probably the Red Cross) were transporting former prisoners of concentration camps who were scattered all over the city of Nordhausen to this location by cars. Soldiers with helmets that had red crosses on the front helped the German civilians carry the dead to a small field on the side of the highway where they were placed in rows next to one another.

When we arrived at this location, I thanked the women for their hospitality, climbed down from the cart, took my jacket and walked towards the farthest building on the right. I stopped for a minute by a group of Germans, who under the supervision of an American soldier, were fussing around the dead and the crippled.

"What happened to your attitude of superiority when only yesterday you considered yourself the super race and regarded the rest of us as rubbish," I yelled out loud in Ukrainian as I turned around to look at them. They turned their heads in my direction, but obviously, they did not understand what I said. So they went back to what they were doing. Now with a subservient attitude, they submitted to the orders of an American soldier who walked among them wielding a wooden stick. I guess the saying, "Power equals might," is true.

I finally arrived at my destination and entered the building since the doors were open. In the first room, as far as I could tell, was a commissary. As I looked around, I saw several dozen prisoners laying on top of the sheets on the floor. It was difficult to watch since many of them were dying and their eyes looked like glass. Some of them from time to time would open their mouths, gasping for air and then moan quietly.

As I walked around the living dead and did not recognize anyone, I entered an adjoining room. I realized that this had been at one time an office. Again, there were corpses laying on the floor and those that were barely alive lay on cots. On the table by the window, I saw a big pile of chocolates and a bunch of cigarettes and some had even fallen on the floor.

"Where did this come from?" I thought and moved towards the table.

A former prisoner started stirring in the cot, lifted his head and shouted in the Ukrainian language, "Stop, don't take anything." I stopped. The prisoner, apparently struggling to overcome his pain, sat up on the cot and propped his back up against the wall. On his chest was the letter "R," for Russian.

"Where are you from?" I asked him.

When he heard my words, he became overjoyed and quickly responded to my query. "How wonderful that you are Ukrainian. I am from Kirovograd. A huge rock hit me in the back when the Americans were bombing the concentration camp near Nordhausen. Many died and with these words, he pointed his hand at those who lay in the room.

"It is so good that you are here. I cannot get up. Hide the chocolates and the cigarettes. Every morning the American nurses bring these items. First, they take a count of all those who are still here, they leave a portion for each person and then after that, they leave. We need to hide everything because if the Americans realize that no one is eating the chocolates then they will not bring us any more."

I realized that my countryman was gripped with the fear of hunger since I myself went through this just weeks ago. I decided to settle in this room for now. At my request, the American nurses removed the corpses so I could remain with my countryman. Then after two weeks, we were informed by the American army that former prisoners who were healthy will be transferred to the concentration camp, "Dora." This will now be the place where all foreigners will be sent so they can eventually be repatriated to their homeland.

CHAPTER 8

The Fate of My Family and Friends

The thought has never left me to find out the fate of my friends who worked with me in the underground and with whom I was arrested in Ukraine and eventually transported to Germany. I was even more interested in the fate of the prisoners that were on the same transport from which I escaped.

I was in the concentration camp Vodokachka in Ukraine with my friends from the underground from December 24, 1942, until we were taken to Buchenwald in separate groups in September 1943. Since I had spent some time in Buchenwald, I knew that most of them had been transported to Dora which was considered one of the worst camps imaginable. I was the only one in my group that was sent to a different concentration camp called Schönebeck, a subcamp of Buchenwald. One and a half years have passed since that time.

For days on end, I would ask all the former prisoners which concentration camps they were in and would give them the names of my friends to see if they knew anything. The answer was always the same. They never heard of them. One day I borrowed a bike from some German man and rode to the train station at Niedersachswerfen. It was only two months ago that these German bandits were transporting me to an unknown destination from this exact location.

As I was walking down the street, I heard someone cry out my name several times. What joy! I put on the brakes of my bike and fell into the arms of my friend Stefan as we hugged each other. He was one of my friends from the underground organization. There were no limits to our joy. My friend Stefan told me

The concentration camp uniform my father was given in Buchenwald that he wore for the next year and a half until his escape to freedom. Notice his prison number 25362 on the front.

that he was evacuated on the same day as I was from this station, Niedersachswerfen. He was with a transport of prisoners from the Dora camp and they were being transferred to northern Germany to be placed in the concentration camp Bergen Belsen. The Germans intended to annihilate several thousand of the prisoners before the area was captured by the Americans.

Then typhus became rampant. Every day hundreds of people died from this terrible disease but Stefan and several of his comrades managed to escape. He had not heard anything about the transport from Rottleberode which was the one I was on. I also found out from him about the death of several of my comrades who were in the Dora camp. On March 3rd, 1945, at 3:00 P.M.

several gallows were erected in the square of the camp and our friends were hanged. An hour later their bodies were burned in the crematorium.

I also received some very sad news about my wife and children. I found out from several sources that they were killed during a bombing raid in Kherson. I was devastated and fell into despair. We were only married four years and I cannot imagine life without her and my children. It was at this point that I decided to change my name, right after the war, to Valentyn Koval. That was my wife's name but instead of Valentina, I made it a masculine name.

Last time my father saw his wife, Valentina,
and his son and daughter at the end of 1942
in Kherson, Ukraine

CHAPTER 9

Dora

Six kilometers to the northwest of Nordhausen stands the concentration camp, "Dora," near the southern Harz Mountains. It was only forest in early 1943 but then the trees were cut down and the construction of an underground weapons factory began, mainly to house and manufacture V-1 and V-2 rockets. The openings to the caves were visible from many places at the foot of these mountains. Dora was enclosed by an electrified barbed-wire fence, with the main entrance located to the east of the camp.

Ten thousand prisoners perished here during the construction of this underground factory. Until the spring of 1944, they were mostly kept underground and deprived of daylight. They worked, slept and ate in these cold, damp tunnels. Most of the prisoners died here and their bodies were transported to Buchenwald to be cremated. However, in 1944, a compound was eventually built above ground to house the prisoners.

The camp commandants forced them to work day and night and as they beat them they shouted, "Hurry up, hurry up." Many of my comrades were transported to this hell hole from Ukraine by the Germans.

A new life has now begun in Dora—the repatriation of foreigners back to their homeland. They are being brought here by the American army from the nearby towns and villages. One hundred forty-four barracks are now filled with the former slaves of Hitler's Germany. Some of the foreigners seem disillusioned with their first days of being liberated. Whereas the Germans, who initially were frightened and worried about their future have slowly regained their composure.

Many of the foreigners such as the Belgians, French, and Italians did not have to wait for an organized transport to their countries. They were eager to leave Germany as fast as they could to get home to their loved ones. Unfortunately, many of the prisoners who were citizens of the Soviet Union were not eager to return. Many of them came from countries such as Ukraine, Belarus, Latvia, etc. who had been under Soviet rule for many decades. Even though outwardly they had great joy over their liberation from the Nazis they were not in a hurry to return and instead were fleeing to the west.

So when the American freight trains arrived at Nordhausen on April 25, 1945, to transfer the former prisoners to Dora, they got indignant and said, "What, again to a concentration camp?" However, after many long discussions with the American officers, some of them agreed to go and left with them.

I was not one of them. My only thought was that I did not want to merge with the masses. I wanted to be alone, go to a village, a farm or even to the mountains. So I decided to visit Dora but with the sole purpose of finding out about the fate of my friends. I went to the camp on foot on the asphalt highway which took me to the foot of the mountains. On both sides of the highway, there was a large accumulation of materials that they used to build the rockets. In plain sight, you could see a rocket in the shape of a cigar made from white metal. The V-2 rocket was twice the size of the V-1 rocket. It was eighteen meters long and one and a half meters in diameter.

The end of the war prevented the Germans from using them in mass against their enemies. The English and American airplanes destroyed the center of Nordhausen, but no bombs were dropped on the warehouses that contained the missile defense weapons. A few months later, all this got into the hands of the Soviets after the Americans left Thuringia.

Before I went into the camp, I walked around the premises and various buildings where the army and the administrative offices were now located. All the documents were destroyed in the political section and I was not able to find the card files of the former prisoners of Dora. Many of the premises were occupied by people who were brought here by the Americans.

Life went on. You could hear people singing or quarreling over a bed as they accompanied me to the main entrance of Dora which was on the east side of the camp. How similar this is to the gates I had to go through every day to the beat of the music of the camp orchestra. Left, left, left, the commandant would shout these same monotonous words when we were assembled for our roll call before they marched us off to forced labor.

To the left and to the right of the gate is a high barbed wire fence. You could hear laughter, singing, music from the radios mingled with the sound of the cars coming through the gate. How so unlike this is from what I had recently experienced.

I walked to the left of the gate alongside the wires. On the concrete pillars, you could still see the emblem of death and the inscription, "Attention, this is a high voltage current." But now there is no current in the wires. The fence is torn in several places which was probably done by the new camp residents. I bypassed the gate since it would be faster to get to the buildings.

The camp already has 30,000 inhabitants. Each of the national groups had their own barracks and the flags of their countries hanging above the doors. Above the roof of the former concentration camp on a high mast was a large Red Star. The Russians have moved their headquarters here.

I learned from some former prisoners of Dora that many of my friends were held in this prison. I went to check out some of the prison cells to see if maybe, they left some sort of inscription. The prison is isolated from the rest of the camp by a high fence. At the entrance of the gate of the prison, stood a Russian soldier with a red star on his sleeve.

I explained to him in broken German that I wanted to look over some of the bunkers. He peered at me with eyes that were red from having drunk too much alcohol, slapped me on the back and let me pass with these words, "Comrade Frenchman, go ahead." I wore a blue French beret so he must have assumed I was French.

As I passed him and looked around, I observed that the Russians lived very well in these headquarters. In a small yard, by the jail, several kitchen units were installed where the women prepared dishes for the comrades who lived here. A terrible argument then ensued between a dozen drunken Russian men. No one paid any attention to me so I went inside the building and stopped in the middle of a long corridor. On both sides of the corridor, there were numerous doors. The cells all looked the same to me as I opened the doors to some of them. In one of the cells, you could hear someone playing the accordion and drunken voices singing.

I opened the door to one of the cells, but it was empty. There was an iron bed attached to the wall, an iron chair and nothing else. My friends must have stayed in one of these cells as I carefully examined the walls. There were inscriptions in different languages from the floor to the ceiling. Among the inscriptions were words of anger, hatred, and curses directed at the German nation and an appeal for their destruction. Others wrote final words of farewell to their homelands and some wrote inscriptions such as, "Long live France," and "Long live Poland."

In one of the cells, was an inscription in the Ukrainian language. "Farewell, my friends!" "Glory to Ukraine." There was no signature underneath. I wonder who wrote those words. I went to another cell, opened the door and saw a man resting in the bed with a bottle of vodka. I closed the door and thought to myself, What is it to them that only recently many people died here.

When I left the corridor, I was stopped by the same drunken Russian soldier with a bottle in his hand. "Hey, my French comrade, let's get drunk."

"I don't understand you," I answered in German.

He cursed at me when I passed by him. I went beyond the gates of the Russian headquarters and breathed a sigh of relief. I stopped at a large square which was west of the main entrance where the prisoners had their roll call every morning. This is the place where they hung my friends. And to the north of the camp, you could see the high chimney from the crematorium. That is where they were burned.

Then someone came up to me and stood right across from me. Suddenly, I heard, "You are alive." This was my Russian friend Peter from Moscow. He was with me in the concentration camp Rottleberode and he also escaped from the transport during the evacuation. He was dressed as a civilian except he wore a red wreath on the left pocket of his jacket. We greeted and embraced one another and with joy squeezed each other's arm. Peter invited me to join him. He seemed to be doing fairly well.

We left the campgrounds and walked to the slope of a steep mountain where we lay in the high fragrant grass. We talked for a long time reminiscing about the past. He then talked about himself and the responsible position he had when he worked for the underground railway in Moscow. He said he was also a member of the Communist party.

Our conversation was interrupted by a group of cheerful young women who apparently were housed nearby. The women spoke in Ukrainian and were well dressed. Modern hairstyles adorned their young faces. But then they started arguing among themselves and glanced in our direction. One of them said, "Let's not quarrel, they may hear us."

Another responded and said, "But they are French and do not understand anything."

Since I did not want to listen to any unpleasant conversations, I approached the girls and asked them what time it was.

Their faces turned red since they knew we had heard what they said. They told me what time it was but then Peter joined us and we all continued talking. It turned out that one of the women, who was Russian was from Kherson, Ukraine which is where I was from. The others were from Kiev, Dnipropetrovsk and other towns in Ukraine.

After a lengthy conversation, one of the women turned to me and said, "We thought you were French. You must be a writer or a journalist."

"What led you to make such an assumption?" I inquired.

"You ask questions about everything," she responded. Then after a short silence, she asked, "What will happen to us? What kind of future awaits us?"

No one answered, then one of the women said excitedly, "There is a dance today at the camp. Let's go, girls."

The girls said their farewells to us and left.

Then Peter lay on the grass and looking up into the sky started sharing about what happened to him. "I was not guilty, I was in the army and got captured. Together with some Germans, we had organized a Communist underground organization and for this, I was sent to a concentration camp. I know that I can't return to Moscow, but if they would allow me to see my family and offered me a job as a janitor, I would be grateful."

I did not answer but was glad that we could share our thoughts with one another. Then we decided to go together the following day to Rottleberode to see if we can obtain any documents and parted ways. However, it would not be easy for me to obtain documents since I was Ukrainian and Ukraine and other countries who were under Soviet rule at that time were not recognized as independent nations. For example, if you lived in the western part of Ukraine, they would only recognize your nationality as Polish and if you lived in the eastern part of Ukraine, you would be considered Russian. Since 1989 most of these nations have regained their national identity and therefore now are considered independent nations with their own language and customs.

CHAPTER 10

Retracing My Steps

I decided that I needed to find out what happened to three of my friends who were with me in the concentration camp Rottleberode. They also escaped from the transport when they were being transferred to the Niedersachswerfen station. I explained this to Peter so together we departed for Rottleberode in the hopes of obtaining our documents and to find out about the fate of my friends.

The sun had come up and you could see that the southern slopes of the Harz Mountains were covered in thick fog. The asphalt highway that we took was wet with dew and shone with the morning rays of the sun. From the city of Kelba to the village of Rottleberode the highway was straight as an arrow. As we got closer we saw a big three-story building covered with red tiles under a steep mountain, north of the village. The building was surrounded with a barbed wire fence and guard towers. You could also see the tattered remains of some of the prisoner's pants that had gotten caught on the wired fence. The prisoners were housed in this building and there was a courtyard between the building and the barbed wired fence that was the roll call area.

We walked through the gate and the door of the building since they were open. Most of the glass in the windows were broken and we noticed that they were all open on the third floor. There was a big stain on the floor the color of dark red. My blood seemed to dry up when I turned to my friend and said, "This is where they shot the sick prisoners." As we continued to look around the large rooms, we saw broken beds, empty boxes that at one time contained canned goods and torn clothes that lay in piles. This had recently been the site of the imprisonment of thousands of people.

The office of the concentration camp was destroyed so trying to find documents here would be useless. We decided to turn to the head of the village and maybe he could at least help us to get some temporary documents. When we made our appearance in the village, the Germans avoided meeting us and disappeared into their houses. We thought we recognized one of the executioners from the concentration camp who was trying to flee from us. We rushed towards him and he stopped when he realized that he could not escape.

"Good day," he greeted us in German and said that he was running away from us because he thought we were Jews. Although he was a prisoner himself, he was known for his cruelty to other prisoners and especially the Jews. He personally killed several hundred people with his club. Before us stood a German parasite, who was used by the Nazis to control the prisoners. He explained that many of the German prisoners, of which he was one, were freed by the Rottleberode commander, Erhard Brauny right before the evacuation from the camps. These thugs assumed that we were all killed so they came to this village to create new documents that would allow them to leave.

He told us he knew nothing about the fate of the prisoners on the transport. We searched him and found a document which he managed to get from the American commanding headquarters. It said that he was Kurt Evert, a political prisoner and so forth and so on.

"Now, look at this," spoke Peter. "It seems that these German bandits lied to the Americans and now they have documents stating that they are political refugees."

We then went to the head of the village and with the testimony of this German bandit, we received documents that proved we were prisoners at the concentration camp Rottleberode. At first, the head of the village resisted, because he did not believe that we stayed in the camp and for what reason. However, the evidence we presented to him convinced him that this was indeed true. The other Germans who were there then fled from the village when they learned of our presence.

In the evening we returned to Nordhausen. As we were walking down the road, an American Patrol was checking documents for those who passed by. We were stopped by an American soldier as he lifted his arm up in the air. We showed him our documents and he allowed us to pass as he waved us through the checkpoint.

We were now in Nordhausen and as I was passing by a street, I noticed a yellow and blue ribbon on the chest of a young man. (These were the colors of the Ukrainian flag.) I could not believe my eyes. I went up to him and asked him, "Are you Ukrainian?"

He looked at me suspiciously and asked, "Who are you."

"I am also Ukrainian," I answered.

We then proceeded to talk for a long time. He informed me that here in Nordhausen, the Ukrainians formed a camp in one of the schools which survived the bombings. He gave me the address and the next day I got some of my other comrades, who had also been prisoners to go to the camp. There were about 800 people with their families crammed into this large school building. The camp was headed by an energetic old professor named Mr. Zlotevsky. He was overjoyed when he learned that former prisoners of German concentration camps came to help.

This camp was like an oasis in the desert that attracted many of the Ukrainians who had also been prisoners in Soviet camps and when the Germans invaded the Soviet Union they transported them to Germany for slave labor. Here, they are not forced to return to their homeland and many of them had fled the Russian centers of repatriation that were established throughout Germany.

I decided with my friend, Stefan to find some Ukrainian organization that could explain to the American authorities to take measures against the Russians not to force their citizens to go back to their homelands. We got the address of the headquarters of the Ukrainian National Association in Hostler which was about eighty kilometers from Nordhausen. We rode on the bicycles which we borrowed and with great difficulty, we arrived at Hostler and found the location of the headquarters.

However, the workers were so frightened that they did not dare speak to us.

Between Hostler and Nordhausen the air went out of my tire just as we had passed one of the villages. I took it off the highway and began to pump air into the tire. Quite by accident, I glanced at a board on the ground with the name of the village Osterhagen. I was surprised that the name of this village was so familiar to me. I stopped pumping and began to remember. All at once I heard someone calling my name. As I turned around towards the sound of the voice, I immediately remembered that this was the same station from where I had escaped during the transport. I barely had enough time to recover from this realization, when I found myself in front of two men who pulled me towards a lovely building near the road.

These were the two Ukrainian men, who fled the same night as I did and from the same cattle car.

"Stay with us for a few days. Join us for dinner since we will be serving borscht (beet soup) and pierogis. After all, you probably have not eaten this for a long time," they said.

Our meeting was so unexpected and intriguing that we decided to stay for a few days. They wheeled the bicycles into the courtyard and went into the house. In the small dining room, the table was already covered and the meal was being prepared by two young women.

I asked who they were and the men responded by saying these were their women. But when their faces turned red and they seemed embarrassed I did not ask any more questions. After they served us the borscht and the pierogis, the men told us how they survived after their escape. I, in turn, told them about my experience. We were sorry that we did not know what happened to the rest of our friends.

I suggested that we go back to the station and find out from the Germans what happened to the transport after our escape.

The men were surprised and asked me, "What station are you talking about?"

"The one right here, Osterhagen," I answered.

As it turned out, they were not aware that this was the same station from which they escaped and here they were living in the village of Osterhagen.

After they escaped, they wandered through the forest for two days and came back to this very same place right around the time it became occupied by the Americans.

Then they told us that when the Americans arrived at this village they got rid of all the Nazis. They appointed a new head of the village and then they contributed on behalf of the German people to set up a small Ukrainian camp behind the village. The camp housed many former prisoners of war. A factory building that manufactured dental prosthesis was confiscated. The owner was not arrested since he was not a Nazi but no one can use the building.

After one of the men had drunk strong wine, he asked me, "What will happen to us now since we may not be able to return to our own country?"

We discussed this problem as we walked back to the Osterhagen train station to revisit the place from where we made our escape.

We learned from the Germans who lived near the station that panic ensued among the SS officers after our escape and the next day the train rode north. I crossed the field to the same forest to which I had fled and found the trunk of the same pine tree which I had embraced and kissed. I decided to carve my initials on the trunk of the tree.

We left the town of Nordhausen behind us and decided to go to Weimar. We came again to an American patrol and were stopped by a soldier with an interpreter so they could check our documents.

We were detained, they took our documents away, were checking something and then they finally let us go. Then Stefan and I decided to go back to the concentration camp Buchenwald to obtain documents about our stay there in 1943. We had already retraced some of our steps so why not use this occasion to continue our journey.

CHAPTER 11

Back to Buchenwald

We went to Buchenwald from Weimar by train. It was about eight kilometers. My heart was beating very rapidly since now we are going there as free men. I remember in the first days when we were brought to this modern, European concentration camp, I was gripped with fear when I saw the thin stream of smoke that ascended to the sky from the tall chimney of the crematorium.

I thought of all the human bodies that were buried in the distance under an infinite web of concentration camp wired fences. How many times I yearned to see my native land as I viewed the landscape surrounded by the high mountains. Hundreds and thousands of prisoners were doomed to death here, where they must have bid farewell to their final days on earth amid this labyrinth of wired fences. I shuddered from the memory of it all.

The train stopped at the railway station of the concentration camp Buchenwald. The foreign masses poured out onto the platform, laughing and talking cheerfully. These are the former prisoners of different nationalities who are waiting for departure to their homeland. They are returning from the city of Weimar to their temporary quarters.

My friend and I stepped onto the platform and as I looked around, it evoked many memories of my time here. Right in front of us was a pile of ruins that was comprised of various devices which were used to produce the missile weapons, especially the V-1 and V-2 rockets.

In May 1944, the American bombers leveled the huge factories and several hundred prisoners were killed. They were the ones who were forced to build these rockets with their own hands and had to work on the machines in the shops. I was also one of the prisoners who had to labor under the brutality of the Nazis to do the same work. The bombs also hit several areas such as the administrative offices of the concentration camp and the private residences of the SS. The slaughtered prisoners were then burned in the crematorium by the Sonderkommando.[1]

The building that housed the records and personal information of the prisoners was also burned down. There was no end to the despair they felt since some had hoped to be released before this happened. And now what? The management of the concentration camp Buchenwald sent out special teams of people (they were also prisoners) to update the information and they had to fill out a questionnaire for each prisoner.

I remember when they came to the concentration camp Rottleberode where I was imprisoned. The Polish

---

1. These were work units made up of German Nazi death camp prisoners, mostly Jews who were forced to dispose of the victims otherwise they would be threatened with death as well.

man[2] they sent to update the documents of the prisoners, told all the Ukrainians you are either Polish or Russian. If you protested, he would slap you in the face and write down whatever he wanted.

We entered the concentration camp and stopped abruptly. I was stunned. We could not believe our eyes. To the left of the gate where the Soviet prisoners of war had at one time been held in a separate Block, over one of the barracks, hung a red flag. There was also a huge portrait of Stalin that hung on the left side of the fence.

That same day, we witnessed the arrival of buses from the Czech Republic who came to take their citizens back to their homeland. They took those who were crippled and sick to sanitariums so they can recover and those who were healthy were taken to their homes in the towns or villages. There was so much joy on the faces of the people who knew they were being taken back to their countries and soon they would be leaving this accursed land.

As we witnessed the departure of many of the foreigners, we felt even more intensely the tragic fate of those who could not go back to their own countries. Many of these countries were not recognized by the Soviet Union and Ukraine was in that category.[3] These were our parting thoughts as we took the last bus to leave Buchenwald. Our desire to obtain documents was not successful because we were told we would have to go back to the Soviet Union to get them.

---

2. I met him again in 1947 as one of the witnesses in Dachau. After that, he went to a university in London.
3. However, on August 24, 1991, Ukraine officially declared itself an independent state and no longer follows the laws of the Soviet Union. They have their own laws, the Ukrainian SSR and their own president.

A Man Without a Country

I left Weimar and went to Augsburg, Germany. But before I got to Augsburg, my certificate from Rottleberode was not accepted by the officer. They confiscated my bicycle, put me in a jeep and I was taken to the military commander's office under custody. There were some American officials in several of the rooms who tried to communicate with me, but without an interpreter, nothing was accomplished.

They finally found a woman who spoke Russian and appeared to be about 30 years old. She worked as an interpreter for the officers in the foreign division. One of the officers who was sitting in a chair, chewing gum, put his legs up on the table. I answered their questions and requested the address of the Ukrainian organization or committee in Augsburg.

The officer examined the papers for a long time, lowered his shoulders and said that there were no Ukrainians in Augsburg. Then he added that he had no choice but to place me in a foreign facility because I did not have the right to travel freely. He decided that I would be better off in the Russian camp and ordered the interpreter to take me there.

As we drove around the streets looking for the Russian camp, I explained to the Americans about the so-called "Soviet paradise" and why their citizens had no desire to go back.

She listened very intently to my explanation and from time to time would ask me questions. Then she inquired, "For what reason were you arrested and forced to stay in a German concentration camp?"

I replied, "For belonging to an underground Ukrainian organization that fought against the Russian and German occupation of Ukraine."

After I spoke these words, she motioned to the chauffeur to stop the car. "Go and look for your people," she said.

I thanked her and as I was getting ready to leave I remembered that they had confiscated my personal items and my bicycle. I told her about this. She wrote down my name and promised to help me. The next day they informed me that I could retrieve my belongings from the military police in the city. The same day I found out that there was a Ukrainian committee and organization in Augsburg located in a partially damaged building.

On September 1945 with the purpose of getting into Switzerland, I arrived in Feldkirch.[1] I encountered many difficulties in obtaining a permit to enter Switzerland from the local French authorities so I turned to another national French organization for help. I met an older woman in uniform who turned out to be a French officer named Kassel. I explained my situation to her but

---

1. The city of Feldkirch is in the western Austrian state of Vorarlberg on the border with Switzerland and Liechtenstein.

she was not able to help me and suggested I go to the Russians for repatriation. We continued talking but our conversation produced no results so I turned around and left the building.

I then decided to turn to the Austrian Association of political prisoners, who were victims of the Nazi German regime. I met a friend in Feldkirch who was with me in Buchenwald so we decided to visit one of their camps. The camp was very similar to a sanitarium and about one hundred people lived here. The former Austrian prisoners seemed very guarded when we came there and the reason for this was revealed almost immediately. I recognized a political prisoner from Block Forty-Four in Buchenwald who had a terrible reputation. We then left the camp since it was obvious we would not receive any help from them.

Despite all these setbacks, we did not lose hope and went to the city of Bregenz, Austria to look for the main headquarters of the French occupation authorities that were governed by the state of Vorarlberg. First, we visited the Swiss consulate. They promised to give me a visa to travel to Switzerland, but only if my request is accepted by the French occupation authorities.

Unfortunately, they denied my request motivated by the fact that I was not a French citizen. Instead, they offered to take me to a repatriation center to wait for deportation to my homeland. I thanked them for their trouble and again told them I cannot go back because I will be executed by the Communists. As we continued to talk I learned that the Chief of the department was also in a German concentration camp. He was involved in the French nationalist movement under the leadership of General De Galle. I proceeded to explain to him who I was and why I could not return to my homeland.

After this, he said to me, "I will give you a referral to an international camp in Hochst near the Swiss border. There is one Ukrainian there and you will be the second one."

The German village of Hochst is located about two hundred meters from the Swiss border. It was surrounded by apple and pear trees. There was such an abundance of fruit on the trees that the weight of it caused the branches to bend downwards. You could also see the high mountains on the Swiss side of the border. I went to the village and sat down on a bench under a large tree to rest.

Here I am a foreigner without any documents and here is another country only a few meters away from me. Two young ladies with baskets sat next to me and to my surprise they spoke in Ukrainian. We started to talk and they told me that in the village in a wooden building there is a Ukrainian camp that housed 500 people. I was told by the Frenchman that I would only be the second Ukrainian in that camp.

The young women brought me to the camp. So I decided to stay there for a few days and acquaint myself with life in the camp. Very quickly I understood the situation and realized why the Frenchman thought there were only two Ukrainians here. Most of the Ukrainians were registered under these nationalities because they were not yet recognized as an independent nation. It truly was an international camp that housed Romanians, Hungarians, Czechs, Poles and many other nationalities.

On the fifth day I decided to take advantage of my "democratic freedom" and without too much delay illegally crossed the Austrian Swiss border. Fate was with me. The night was dark, it was raining heavily and the howling wind protected me. The French and Swiss border guards were fast asleep at their posts as I crossed the border without being detected.

CHAPTER 13

Life in a Displaced Persons Camp

It was dark when I crossed the border into Switzerland. I had to find some shelter since it was raining and very windy. I managed to stumble across an abandoned shed where I spent the night. In the morning as I ventured out I picked a few apples and pears from the numerous trees that grew in the surrounding area. I needed to devise a plan to obtain travel or work documents so I can travel freely and eventually find some gainful employment. I had numerous conversations with the residents of the camp that I visited in Austria and was informed that there are Ukrainian camps for Displaced Persons. There is a camp that is being organized in Augsburg, Germany which is in the American zone which I preferred since I always had a longing to eventually immigrate to America. There you can be free and live according to your beliefs.

Since my efforts to obtain documents were not successful with the Swiss consulate or the Austrian Association of Political Prisoners I decided to turn to the Red Cross. I did not want to go to the German Red

Cross but decided to go to the French since they may be more sympathetic to my plight. But where are they located and how will I get there?

Then I realized that my mother had relatives in Zurich and they might be able to help me. Zurich was not far from the border, maybe 120 kilometers. I should be able to reach them since I remembered their address or I can make inquiries once I get there. However, I needed to exercise great caution so as not to be pulled aside by any military officers or policemen. After all, I was a man without a county, with no identification and could be forcibly repatriated to the Soviet Union.

Maybe a train would be the best way to get there, but they may ask me for some identification when I go to purchase the ticket. So I decided to walk in the direction of Zurich along the highway but would hide among the trees so I couldn't be detected. The countryside was beautiful and you could see the snow-covered mountains in the distance.

It took me several days to reach Zurich by foot, although I did accept a ride from a stranger and was driven a short distance. I located the street and the number of the residence of my relatives. They were very surprised to see me, especially my mother's aunt who was quite elderly and a married cousin with his family. They had heard about the death of my wife and children so were relieved to see that I was still alive.

They lived in a modest, comfortable house and my mother's aunt made haste to prepare a meal for me. When we all sat at the table, I explained my situation to them and the events that had transpired in my life for the last few years. They were very sympathetic to my plight and agreed to help me find a French Red Cross center. However, that may require a trip to Geneva where the headquarters of the French Red Cross was located. It was about 278 kilometers from Zurich and would take about three to four hours, but they can arrange transportation for me so I can get the required documents. The French Red Cross was more lenient in giving work or travel permits since they had more compassion for the prisoners who did not want to be repatriated.

The reason many were unwilling to return to their countries, especially the Soviet citizens was that freedom of speech, religious expression, and other democratic rights were suppressed in the Soviet Union. Those who were forcibly repatriated faced certain death or imprisonment. Many were either killed, tortured or sent to Siberia where they were worked to death in the Soviet prison camps.

My cousin purchased tickets for us to take the train to Geneva. When we arrived, he located the headquarters of the French Red Cross and accompanied me to their office. We met with the President of the Red Cross for the Stateless (or those without a country) and they issued me a certificate of registration that will now allow me to travel freely and even obtain work (see next page).

We took the train back to Zurich and I was so grateful that this time my efforts to obtain documents were successful after being denied multiple times. My relatives invited me to spend a few weeks with them which I did before I went back to Germany. I needed to get established in a community so I can begin to rebuild

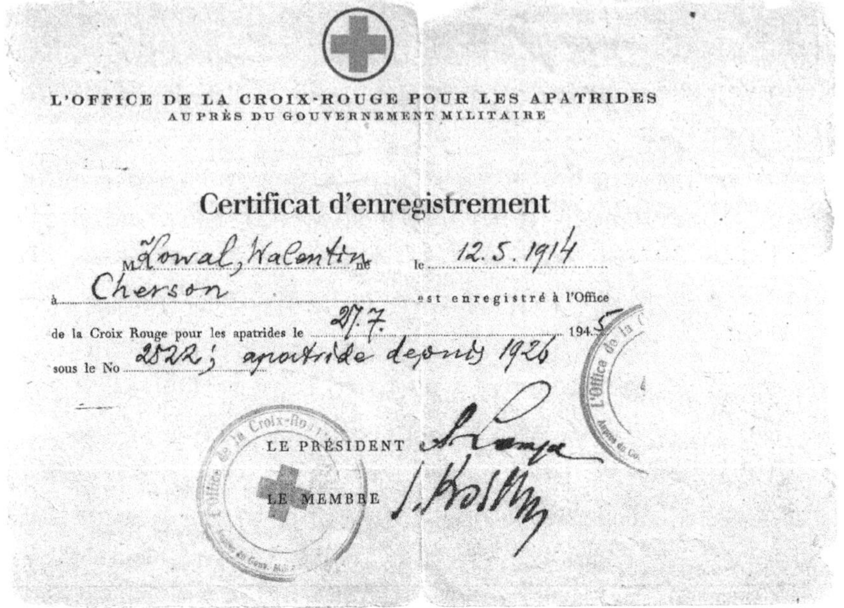

Translation:

The Office of the Red Cross for the Stateless
along with the military government
Certificate of registration
Mr. Kowal, Valentin born the 12th of May 1914
at Cherson registered at The Office
of the Red Cross for the Stateless the 27th of July 1945
under the Number 2822; stateless since 1926
The President (signature)
The Member (signature)

my life after all the suffering and torment that I had endured in the last three years.

After having spent some time with my relatives in Zurich, they put me on a train to Bregenz, Austria where I entered legally on September 30, 1945.

Augsburg was only 160 kilometers from Bregenz so I took a train there and after making some inquiries located a Ukrainian Displaced Persons Camp called Somme-Kaserne. It was one of the largest camps and had between 2000-5000 people residing there. I decided to make my residence here and get involved in the community. I went to the administrative office to register and arrange living accommodations. The UNRRA (the United Nations Relief and Rehabilitation Administration) was running many of the camps although the military took an active role by providing many services, such as security and transportation.

The living quarters in the camp were old German army barracks and old school buildings, but for now, it will have to suffice. I was directed to one of the barracks and settled in but I was plagued with the fear of repatriation and uncertainty about the future. Since this camp is in the zone that comes under the authority of the Americans I can always reason with them if the Soviets try to force me to go back.

There must be a cafeteria or storehouse where you can purchase food. I also need to find out what kind of organizations have been established here and whether I can locate some of my friends.

The next day as I walked throughout the camp I saw buildings that were partly destroyed but at the same time, there was much activity and crowds of people going to and fro. The landscape still showed the ravages of war and much of the area was unkempt. There were bushes and trees that needed to be trimmed and grass that could use a gardener's touch. But with so many other immediate concerns such as shelter, food, and medicine who cared about these trivial matters.

Immersed in my thoughts, I kept walking and heard someone call out my name. As I turned around, I was amazed to see my friend, Oleksa, an old political colleague of mine from many years ago. We embraced one another and Oleksa excitedly told me of all the organizations that were being established here, especially the political and literary groups. He informed me that mutual friends of ours were also here and there are a lot of opportunities to get involved in the community.

There was a need for an editor at the editorial and publishing office of the Ukrainian newspaper, "Ukrainska Duma." He took me to their office and within a short

My father and his friend Oleksa

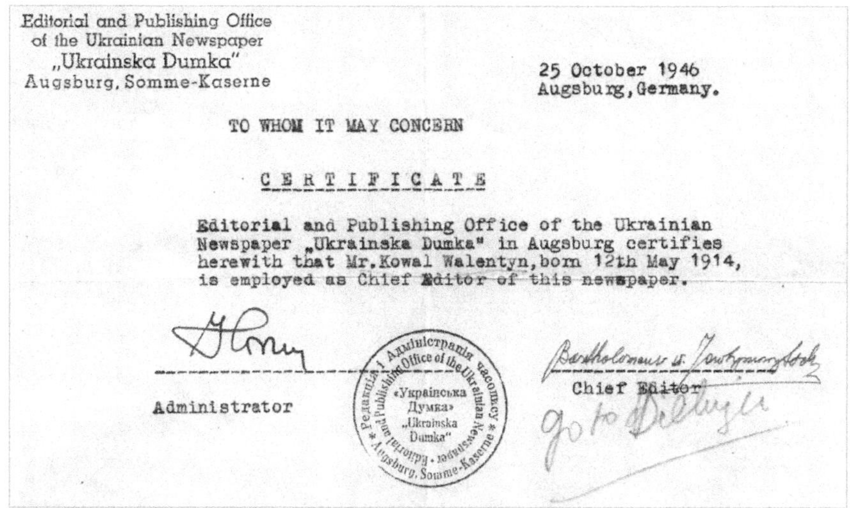

A certificate of my father's employment as Chief Editor of a Ukrainian newspaper in the Somme-Kaserne Displaced Persons Camp in Augsburg

amount of time, I became the Chief Editor of this publication. I also found out that schools had already been established and many cultural and social organizations were being formed. We talked at length about our lives and practical ways we can contribute to the Ukrainian community at this camp. We decided to look for our friends and discuss with them the different ideas we had about forming an association for the youth. I was particularly interested in publishing articles of a political and literary nature. Despite the uncertainty of our future, we felt that at least for now, we had a purpose and could work together for a common cause. I still had the hope that someday my dream of going to America would be realized and that I could live as a free man without any fear or dread of being imprisoned for my beliefs.

As we bonded together as a community, vocational schools, sports clubs, music and drama groups were eventually set up. I spent many days, weeks, and

My father (second from right) with his journalistic and literary friends in Somme-Kaserne

My father (far left) with fellow journalists at a committee meeting.

months discussing topics of interest with my political and literary comrades. During some of our social events, I met a lovely woman, named Tatiana who had a child from a previous marriage. Her husband had been a pilot but was killed during one of his missions. She was also from Ukraine but had experienced much hardship during the war and ended up at this camp. She was very beautiful and had many suitors of which I

My father met my mother at the Ukrainian Displaced Persons Camp Somme-Kaserne in Augsburg, Germany, in 1947

was one. Because food was scarce you courted a woman by bringing her extra food and those who provided the most were given priority. I fought for her attention any way I could and found ways to obtain extra food. But I did not give up and persevered in the hopes that I would gain her affection.

Meanwhile, the Soviets were still going to the different camps demanding that their citizens be forcibly repatriated. The Ukrainians particularly resisted repatriation and submitted complaint letters to the Allied authorities. They even staged protests such as anti-repatriation campaigns and even requested political asylum. However, by the end of 1945, forcible repatriations were not allowed anymore in the US zone. Then the IRC (International Refugee Organization) took over the administration of the DP camps around June 1947.

A political gathering at a Displaced Persons Camp

A youth gathering at a Displaced Persons Camp

CHAPTER 14

Only Two Witnesses

The years passed and the memory of the tragic times I experienced started to fade with the cares and concerns of daily life. Sometimes when I am at work, I think of my friends and how much I miss them. How empty life is without them when I think of their bravery and strength of spirit. How is it possible that the 2000 prisoners that were evacuated from Rottleberode disappeared without a trace?

On August 15, 1947, at the Ukrainian Displaced Persons camp Somme-Kaserne in Augsburg, where I was residing, the Americans appeared and invited any former prisoners of the German concentration camps to the theatre. They bought photos of the German criminals and Hitler's executioners who were caught, arrested and under investigation by the American military court in Dachau. The photos were glued to cardboard panels and arranged on the tables in the hall.

I looked with agitation at each face of the SS officers, to see if I recognized any of them from the different concentration camps I was imprisoned. As I looked at one of the photos, I recognized the commander of the concentration camp Rottleberode, Erhard Brauny and then two more: Paul Maischein who was a medical aide and Walter Ulbricht who was a clerk. I thought to myself, how it is possible that those who were responsible for transporting thousands of prisoners to their deaths are still alive. The Americans told me that I will receive a summons to go to Dachau before long, to be a witness at the trial of these criminals. I also had to sign a protocol document that I recognized them and will be present at the trial. On September 15, 1947, I received the summons to go to Dachau.

I took a train to Munich-Dachau but was somewhat distraught since the memory of the recent past flashed through my mind. I wanted to find out about the fate of my friends. Are they alive or did they perish?

At the gate of the former concentration camp, the American guard gave me a pass. Then I was taken by truck to a specified address. We rode on a wide asphalt highway and along the highway was a high wired fence. To the left of the highway were offices and garages. After they checked my pass and all the formalities were taken care of, I was guided to the hotel in the town. The American soldier then gave me a ticket for the dining room, a package of American tobacco and directed me to my room in the hotel.

Many people of different races and nationalities were staying at the hotel. All of them were former prisoners of the German concentration camps and now they will be witnesses at the trial. There were eight American military courts working every day to review the cases before them of crimes perpetrated by the German officers against the prisoners of the different concentration camps.

On arrival, I had a free day and decided to get acquainted with the camp. I went to see the crematorium. It was in a small courtyard protected by a high brick wall. In the middle of the courtyard was a large building with a low square shaped chimney. The crematorium.

There was a terrible stench in the courtyard. These were the decomposed bodies which were buried near the stoves and discovered by the American troops when they occupied the concentration camp in 1945. At the entrance of the crematorium, there was something written in the English language on a board and the numbers–238,000. This indicated the number of people who were burned here by the Germans.

I looked over the equipment and saw two large furnaces for burning corpses. There were remnants of ashes and pieces of bones. I saw heavy steel doors to the left that led to the gas chambers. There were quite a few shower faucets suspended from the ceiling from which gas was released. The supply of gas was controlled by means of two valves which the operator would release and watch from the observation window.

It is difficult to imagine how a person could watch people who were expecting to take a shower and then calmly unscrew the valves to let in the deadly gas. There was also a room further down that contained special instruments of torture. The Germans not only killed the prisoners with gas but they also shot them in the head. Behind the crematorium near a high wall between the bushes was a pile of sand which was overgrown with grass. This was the gravesite of those who had been executed and you could see the dried-up wreaths and the red ribbons which were placed here. There was also something written in German on the red ribbons. Something to the effect of the eternal memory of fighters.

From the courtyard of the crematorium, there is a gate that leads to hundreds of dog cages that are perfectly arranged in rows. The dogs were kept in these cages to protect the camp, but they were also used to chase after the prisoners if they tried to escape. The cages now stand empty and are a sad reminder of times past. I left the crematorium very depressed and downcast.

On the other side of the highway was the actual concentration camp near a deep moat. I saw the high watchtowers where the guards with their machine guns had been stationed and the high wired fences which at that time had electric currents that were operational. How ironic that the Germans who were guilty of all these crimes against humanity are now residing here.

The next day after breakfast I presented myself before the investigator who oversaw the case against the criminals from Rottleberode. We got somewhat acquainted with one another and he asked me in the German language if I will need an interpreter and in what language. I said I am Ukrainian and then asked him if he knew what happened to the prisoners who were transported from Rottleberode.

He answered that everyone perished in Gardelegen. This news was very painful for me since many of my friends were on that transport. Then the investigator said that they were only able to find two witnesses from the whole transport—me and a Polish man. The Polish man had already given his testimony, now it was my turn. We approached the board which had the photos of the three criminals from Rottleberode and I pointed them out to the investigator.

The investigator left to search for an interpreter, but it is probably unlikely they will find someone who speaks Ukrainian. I was getting impatient waiting for the investigator to return, but was curious about the other witness and wondered if I knew him personally. Maybe I could learn from him in more detail about the death of my friends.

I decided to look around the room while I waited for the investigator. Soldiers were sitting and thumbing through papers at six different tables. They were the investigators who would be prosecuting the various cases. Two young German women with painted lips and nails were pounding on the typewriters. The room was messy and very dirty and papers were scattered everywhere in piles on the tables, on the window sills and on top of the closets. The current witnesses if they so desired, had the right to examine the documents and make any notations on the papers.

The investigator showed up after a half hour and said that there was no one in Dachau that could interpret in Ukrainian but they would have to find someone who spoke Russian. So meanwhile, due to the lack of an interpreter, my testimony was postponed. I excused myself and went to look for the Polish witness. Just as I passed the corridor, the court was taking a break. All the defendants were taken outside to the courtyard. Among them, I recognized the former criminals of Rottleberode.

They all looked extremely well–laughing, lighting up their cigarettes.

In the corridor, the wives and close relatives of the criminals sat on the benches. The wife of the commandant of the concentration camp Dachau who was sentenced to death by hanging even dined in the same restaurant as the witnesses and the administrative staff.

I finally found the other Polish witness in one of the hotel rooms. We immediately recognized one another. I operated a lathe and he worked as an electrician in one of the shops at Rottleberode. His name was Romuald Bak. He was a Polish Jew from Warsaw. He told me what had happened to the prisoners that were on the same transport from which I escaped at the Osterhagen station. Since many of them were close friends of mine I was eager to know the outcome of their fate

CHAPTER 15

The Tragedy of Gardelegen

On April 8, 1945, the train with the transport of 1400 prisoners from Rottleberode, Stampeda, Ilfeld and Ellrich arrived at Mieste on April 9th from Osterhagen. They languished in the railway yard another 3 days and were told that the Americans were only thirteen kilometers away. However, when a bomb fell in the railway yard, the SS took off and the prisoners scurried in all different directions. Those who had gotten away were hiding in the bushes and in the forest. The US troops still had not arrived so the Germans mobilized the Hitler youth, the local leadership in the villages and any German soldiers that were in the area to capture the fugitives.

As the prisoners were rounded up, many of them were shot, but others were tricked into believing that they would be turned over to the Americans. By this method of deception, the Germans herded over 1000 prisoners into a large barn where they were burned alive and some were shot trying to escape.

I was grief stricken to find out that most of my comrades had been murdured and this is the fate that would have awaited me if I had not jumped off the boxcar in Osterhagen. He then told me that before the Germans had time to bury all the bodies, the American army arrived at the site in Gardelegen on April 14th. The crime scene was horrifying. The Americans were shocked by what they saw and wanted to make sure it was made known to the world. After taking photographs and hearing the testimony of eyewitnesses, the US military authorities issued an order to the civilian German population to prepare a cemetary for the slaughtered prisoners.

Close to 1016 people died in a barn by the airfield in Gardelegen. A large cemetary was erected near the barn and 1016 of the victims were to be buried in the individual graves. The Americans had the townspeople dig the graves, inter the bodies, and erect a white cross or a Star of David over each grave. Amond the dead were Poles, Russians, Ukrainians, Jews, Frenchmen, and many other nationalities.

I had always hoped that someday soon I would see some of my comrades again and we would continue our work advancing the cause of freedom. But I realized that I will never see them again and will have to adjust to the emptiness of not having them in my life anymore.

Gardelegen is now a national memorial that is located at the scene of the massacre. It is a reminder of the 1016 concentration camp prisoners who were murdered there in a field barn on April 13, 1945. There is also a Memorial Cemetery where the victims are buried.

CHAPTER 16

The Trial

The next morning, I went back again to present myself before the investigator. He informed me that they have found an interpreter who knows the Ukrainian language. He picked up the telephone handle and dialed a number. I sat by a table that was not being used and started browsing through the papers. I came upon the matter of Gardelegen among the many different protocols and confessions. It was typed in the English language and substantiated with many photos.[1] There were also some protocols written in Polish and among them, I recognized the testimony of the Polish man Bak.

The interpreter finally came and we began to acquaint ourselves with one another. But after speaking a few words it turns out that he does not know the Ukrainian language but only understands it. I did not want to disappoint the investigator and agreed with the interpreter that I would speak to him in Russian but if they ask what language I am speaking, he would reply Ukrainian. To be sure that he was trustworthy, I decided

---

1. The Nordhausen war crimes trial held before the US military court at Dachau in 1947. It is also referred to as the Dachau Dora trials.

to get to know him a little better. This was important to me since he was going to translate my testimony into German for the defendants and another interpreter will translate from German into English for the court.

I asked him what was his nationality, how does he know the Russian language and what can he tell me about Ukraine. Without hesitation, the interpreter said that he is a German from the Czech Republic and he took special courses to study the Russian language. During the German occupation of Ukraine in 1942, he was an interpreter in the office of the military commandant in the city of Skadovsk, Ukraine. He was also very knowledgeable about the long-standing hostility between the Russians and the Ukrainians. As a result, I was completely satisfied with the interpreter.

After we got acquainted, we dispersed so that the next day, as the investigator said, I will be prepared to give my testimony. The interpreter departed but I reviewed the documents further on the table, with the permission of the investigator. There were several dozen thick books filled with the names of the German criminals from minor government officials to the heads of concentration camps. Their movements and activities were recorded with exceptional accuracy as well as characterizing the personal attributes of each SS official. Because of these lists, the German criminals were subject to exposure and all this has been disclosed to the court.

The next day I arrived at the courtroom and met with my interpreter. There was an American soldier guarding the front door of the courtroom. My interpreter and I had to wait in the corridor until we were summoned.

I was anxious because they will soon call me to the courtroom where they are prosecuting the criminals. My testimony must be substantiated and not challenged. I must prove that these criminals were guilty of committing these crimes, even before my very eyes since I, myself was a victim.

The Americans cautioned us that they need facts, not just generalizations so that the prosecutor's office will have grounds to demand the highest punishment for the defendants. The bandits tried to defend themselves by not acknowledging their complicity in these crimes, but instead, put the blame on those who have not been caught yet or have already been executed without a trial. The criminals were certain that none of the prisoners had survived and with the help of the German prosecutors could easily contest the veracity of one or two witnesses. I tried to remember even the minutest moments of my life in the concentration camp Rottleberode. I then recalled the details of the crimes committed by three of the defendants–Erhard Brauny, Paul Maischein, and Walter Ulbricht.

The doors opened and a soldier stepped onto the threshold and called out my name. I entered the courtroom with my interpreter. I was told to take a seat on a high chair in front of a long table where the American judges were sitting. My interpreter sat next to me on the left. On the right side sat a Polish man who translated the testimony into the English language.

The judges quietly conferred among themselves. Under the wall on the left was a platform where eighteen of the criminals stood and everyone had a board on his chest with a serial number. There was a whole row of German defendants in front of the criminals. On the opposite side to the right sat the American investigators and prosecutors. Two stenographers were preparing to record the course of the trial on special machines.

The judges got up from their seats and then everyone stood up. Then the senior chairman of the court starts speaking in English. "This does not apply to you," explained my interpreter.

The judges then sat down and everyone occupied their own seats.

Then the prosecutor turned to me (through the interpreter). "Stand up," said the interpreter, "Raise your right hand and put your two fingers together like this," as he demonstrated to me, and say, "I swear to tell the truth."

I repeated after him, "I swear to tell the truth."

"You swore to the court that you would only speak the truth," explained the interpreter.

The court, "Please approach the defendants and point your finger at all those whom you recognize."

I approach the criminals. "Bandit Erhard Brauny, the commander of the concentration camp Rottleberode," I spoke loudly pointing my finger at him.

Without the slightest sign of anxiety, the bandit turned over the board with the numbers on his chest.

After a few minutes, I look closely at his face. I looked at the others and they all appeared to be well fed.

"Bandit Walter Ulbricht—the accountant for the concentration camp Rottleberode." I declared, pointing my finger at the second bandit. "Bandit Paul Maischein— the physician for the concentration camp Rottleberode,"

Those who I named just kept fidgeting with their boards. After I identified the criminals, I returned to my own seat.

The court requested, "Tell the court everything you know about the criminals that you identified."

I stood as I testified before the American court and I paused several times to allow the translators enough time to interpret accurately in two languages.

"Dear Honorable Members of the Court! I, along with the other prisoners of which many of them died in the massacre at Gardelegen, were treated as sub-humans and slaves. We had to wear an OST patch which marked us as workers from the East. (Osterbeiter) I had to operate a lathe twelve hours a day in a dark underground dungeon about 100 meters in depth. We did not have enough food, clothing or adequate medical care. Many of the prisoners died from exhaustion and were brutally beaten, especially the Jewish prisoners. Erhard Brauny was often drunk and shot at the prisoners every night, and Kapo Ulbricht also participated in the mistreatment and brutality toward the prisoners."

"Before I continue I wanted to point out that the SS were not the only ones responsible for these criminal activities. The German civilian population also took an active part in the capturing and killing of the prisoners when they hid in the forest during the evacuation of the Rottleberode camp. I know for a fact that on April 9, 1945, five prisoners who were hiding in the forest were killed by German civilians near the village of Stempeda."

The German defense team interrupted my speech at this point and yelled, "The witness is not speaking what is relevant to this trial. We protest against his accusing and blaming the whole German nation."

Then the prosecution team came forward and turned to the defense team and explained, "The witness has the right to speak all that he knows about this case."

Around six o'clock in the evening, I finished my testimony against the three criminals that were on trial. Then I had to answer questions for two more hours from the German defense team and was cross-examined by the court. The defense team tried to trip me up with minor details but my answers were concise and clear which put them in a compromising position. At eight o'clock in the evening, the court session ended. The investigator made it clear that the criminals will be sentenced to death by hanging. I did not wait for the verdict of the court but decided to leave Dachau.

I later found out that Erhard Brauny was sentenced to life imprisonment and eventually died at the Landsberg prison in 1950 from cancer. Walter Ulbricht and Paul Maischein were only sentenced to five years in prison.

CHAPTER 17

New Life in America

Written by Valentyn's daughter Oxana

My father left Dachau after the trial around the end of September 1947 and went back to Augsburg to Somme-Kaserne to continue his life there. He lived there until the middle of 1948 and then moved to Munich around that time and resided in the Displaced Persons camp there called Werner-Kaserne. He was offered a position as the head of the press department of the League of Ukrainian Political Prisoners.

While he was at the camp, President Truman had signed The Displaced Persons Act on June 25, 1948. It allowed hundreds of thousands of Displaced Persons to enter the United States within the next two years. My father requested political asylum and applied for permission to enter the United States. He arrived at Ellis Island in early 1950 and decided to live on the lower East Side of Manhattan.

In the meantime, he made inquiries about Tatiana, who left Germany about six months earlier to the United States. They lost contact with one another because of circumstances beyond their control, but he found out that she was working as a maid in Boston for a wealthy family. He immediately went to Boston and once he located her whereabouts, he asked her to marry him. At first, she hesitated but he responded by saying, "Do you want to be a maid here for the rest of your life?" So she accepted his proposal, they went back to New York and got married at the Municipal Office Building in Manhattan. Soon after that, I was born and then two years later they moved to Brooklyn where my younger brother was born.

It was not easy to adjust to life in a country that did not speak your language. However, so many Ukrainians had immigrated by then to New York City that they were assimilated into the community within a very short time. Many of my father's political friends had also immigrated to New York so they did not waste any time establishing youth, political and literary organizations. My father worked at odd jobs until a few years later he got a position as a brazier and then a draftsman.

Outside of work, he became the editor of a publication called, Mission of Ukraine, which was a division of the Association for the Liberation of Ukraine. He also became very active in a group called Americans to Free Captive Nations. He was also a member of the American Security Council, the political board of the Ukrainian-American Congress Committee and the Ukrainian-American Journalist Association. This was all voluntary and he never received any monetary compensation for all his activities. He eventually became an American citizen in 1957 and my mother as well.

Every year there would be a demonstration on Liberty Island by the Americans to Free Captive Nations and nations who were under bondage would participate to show their support.

My father was passionate about seeing all nations liberated from bondage and oppression since he had lived under the Communist yoke most of his life and then was a slave to the Nazi regime for three years while being forced to work in the underground tunnels. So he continued the work he had started in Ukraine and in Germany and his passion never abated even to the end of his life.

Then in the early 1980s, he found out that his first wife and two children were still alive and living in the city of Kherson, Ukraine. Throughout the years he continued to make inquiries about his family but his attempts to locate them were unsuccessful. He knew they were killed during the war according to the information he received, but there is always the possibility that they somehow may have survived. He met a woman who was visiting the United States from Ukraine and he asked her to go in person to that city to see what she could find out. When she returned, she made some inquiries about his family and located their current address. She knocked on the door and his first wife opened the door. She explained who she was and when his first wife, Valentina found out that Anatoli was still alive, she fainted.

Once she came to herself they had a lengthy conversation about the events that transpired during the

Demonstrations staged by "Americans to Free Captive Nations"
over the course of several years

Another demonstration by the Americans to Free Captive Nations. My father is on the left.

war. Apparently, she had been told that her husband had died in the concentration camp and she barely got out alive with her two children, from her home which was destroyed. She had only been married four years to my father and now it was almost thirty-eight years later. She managed to survive, got married again and had another child.

My father and his first wife began to correspond with one another and sent each other updated photos. By this time, my mother had died and Valentina's second husband had also died. My father sent her an invitation to visit the United States with his two children who were grown by now. Unfortunately, she was afraid to come because the cold war had not yet ended so they never saw one another again in person.

However, I had the opportunity to meet his first wife and my-half-brother and sister in 1991 after the Berlin wall fell and then it became easier to travel to the Soviet Union. Unfortunately, my father had died two years earlier from Alzheimer's and Valentina died a few years after my first visit to Ukraine. I was able to communicate with them since I did speak Ukrainian, otherwise, it would have been difficult because none of them spoke English.

I visited them several times in the 1990s and we kept in touch via letters and phone calls. My half-brother came to visit us in the United States in 2006 for several weeks by our invitation. They are all quite elderly now so we don't communicate that often anymore.

In conclusion, I would like to share some of the principles that my father practiced that caused him to survive the Holocaust and fulfill his purpose in life.

CHAPTER 18

Principles My Father Practiced Overcoming Adversity

There are seven principles my father practiced that enabled him to overcome his adverse circumstances. I will elaborate on each principle in more detail and as you follow them I believe it will help you to overcome and even triumph amid your circumstances.

The most important principle is having a VISION for your life, "For without a vision the people perish."[1] Vision gives you purpose which is the second principle, but we will discuss that later. Some people are very fortunate that they find their passion early in life, others may find it much later, but it is never too late. My father was fortunate that he discovered his vision early in life, which was to see not only Ukraine but other captive nations living in total freedom, pursuing their passions without any oppressive interference from the Communists. Then when the Nazis took over Eastern Europe, his fight for freedom took on another front and he paid a heavy price for his beliefs.

---

1. Proverbs 29:18.

When you have a vision for your life, it is always better to strive for objective rather than ego-centric goals. There is a greater sense of fulfillment and satisfaction when your focus is directed toward the greater good of others and not just what benefits you can gain. In my father's case he always kept that vision in the forefront and did not consider his own comforts nor did he look for any monetary compensation.

Does your vision consume you to the point where everything else is secondary and would you be willing to die for what you believe if you ever had to make a choice? I am not advocating neglecting your work or families. My father held a steady job to make a living and supported his family. However, in his spare time, he dedicated all his efforts to his vision and worked tirelessly to see it come to pass.

To quote the words of Nietzsche, "He who has a Why to live for can bear almost any How." The prisoners who did not have a vision for their life were usually the first ones to give up. Lack of hope and no vision for his future caused my father's friend Pawel to sink into despair. He spoke of death, giving up and surrendering to the Nazis. My father, on the other hand, refused to succumb to those thoughts and with all the strength he could muster, spoke words of life. When everything is taken away from you, you still have the freedom to decide how you will respond to a situation. "Death and life are in the power of the tongue,"[2] so the more you speak words of life, the better your outcome. Viktor E. Frankl wrote, "Man's inner strength may raise him above his outward fate."[3]

---

2. Proverbs 18:21.
3. Excerpt from, "Man's Search for Meaning," by Viktor E. Frankl who survived Auschwitz and three other concentration camps.

The second principle is having a PURPOSE. Once you have a vision for your life, then you can identify your purpose and the reason for your existence. Once that is established you can work towards validating your purpose and pursuing it with every fiber of your being. My father was passionate about his purpose: To fight with whatever means he had at his disposal, in his case, the power of the pen and staging demonstrations so every captive nation could be free from bondage, whether it was Communism or any other ism. Every day this was foremost in his mind, even though his future was uncertain along with the other prisoners who were in the concentration camps.

The uncertainty of not knowing when and if liberation will come, must have taken a toll on those who were interned in these camps and many who lost hope would resort to suicide. Some of the prisoners would run into the electrified barbed-wire fences because death seemed to be an easy way out since the odds of survival were rather poor. The cramped living quarters that should have slept only a few hundred would house close to a thousand. Also, the thought life constantly revolved around food since there was such a lack of it until eventually, the body would begin to devour itself.

Under these conditions, a person would have to have an inner strength and resolve to go on. Since all the prisoners were subject to the same conditions, those who felt that they had a purpose to fulfill would forge ahead despite the weakness of their bodies. They were certain that they had concrete tasks waiting to be accomplished in the outside world. It must have taken every ounce of strength to live day after day not knowing what fate awaited you in the camps.

However, in my father's case, it was not just surviving the camps, but what happened after the camps. Escaping during the transport into the forest, wandering for days starving and weak from hunger and having to hide from the German soldiers. His desire to live and accomplish his purpose dominated his whole psyche which gave him that inner strength to go on. He also did not just think about himself but also looked out for his friend Pawel and tried to save him as well.

Purpose in life is a motivating force which will propel you to accomplish your goals and lead you to your desired haven. However, the third step we will discuss is having a plan. You cannot fulfill your purpose without executing a plan of action as to how you will get there.

The third principle is having a PLAN. You cannot fulfill your purpose unless you have a plan on how to get there. In my father's case, he was already planning on how to escape from the concentration camp when he arrived there. Although circumstances were such that his plan to escape was realized when he jumped from the cable car and ran into the forest. He then had to plan how to survive in the forest while escaping from the Nazis. After that, he had to plan how to get documents so he could travel freely and eventually get work.

When he immigrated to the United States years later, he was already planning how to fight for the independence of Ukraine and the other captive nations. He was the co-founder of a Ukrainian youth organization, wrote articles for different publications, became active in different associations and even helped stage demonstrations against nations who had oppressive regimes. His passion was without limits and many hours into the night I would hear the banging of the typewriter keys while he wrote articles for various newspapers. Sometimes when there were demonstrations, he would create placards to be carried by different individuals. His planning and activities produced great results that it even caught the attention of the media. Eventually, he was interviewed on television in the early '50s where he was able to talk about his political and journalistic work.

If you focus, which is the fourth principle, on your purpose and vision, and do it for unselfish reasons, you will eventually gain the attention of others. However, that should not be your main motivation. Always keep in mind the needs of others and how this would benefit them in their current situation.

The fourth principle is FOCUS. Planning without a focus will cause you to be distracted easily from your purpose. There are many things vying for your attention and it takes great resolve to complete the task at hand. There were no internet or cell phones when my father was alive so it may have been easier to focus on his purpose. In our current society, we have so much more to distract us that it would take great effort and commitment to focus on accomplishing the tasks we were commissioned to do.

When my father was escaping from the Nazis in the forest, he was so focused on not being caught by the soldiers that he realized even sleep would be a detriment to his survival. In other words, he did whatever it took to ensure a good outcome so that he would not be another statistic. Even though most of us are not facing imminent death, we can learn from this example that focus is the key to ensuring a good outcome in any of our endeavors. We will also achieve the desired results in a shorter amount of time and not waste a lot of time on tasks that do not contribute to our overall purpose.

The fifth principle is PERSEVERANCE. If we are truly convinced of our vision and purpose we will persevere despite obstacles and hindrances that will inevitably come our way. At this point, many give up pursuing their vision and purpose because, in their own minds, the process of getting there seems impossible to attain.

In the camps, many gave up because of the thought of having to endure years of labor, hunger, beatings, and hardship with no knowledge of when and if liberation would come was beyond their capacity to accept. Granted it would be hard for anyone to accept the uncertainty of not knowing when their suffering would be over. It may have been easier if they knew that on such and such a date we will be liberated and our slavery will end.

In my father's case, he had no inkling of when he would be liberated from the camps but his vision and purpose for his life was the reason he persisted despite the hardships. Even when he escaped from the transport and had to wander through the forest, he had no guarantee that he would not eventually be captured by the Nazis. But he persevered, even though his body was weak from hunger, using only his wits, not only to save himself but to try to save his friend Pawel as well.

The desire to see your vision and purpose become a reality in your life requires great effort and perseverance.

You must desire it very strongly otherwise your tendency will be to give up and not move forward. Hopelessness and despair prevailed in the camps since it was very difficult to see any redemptive purpose to all their suffering. Many questioned if there was a meaning to all this suffering. My father, along with the other inmates could not understand what they did to deserve this kind of treatment but how they responded to their situation strengthened their inner life even though the outward circumstances were intolerable. Those who continued to have hope and the belief that this will all come to an end soon were able to endure the hardships. Others gave up hope and could not visualize their future anymore outside of the camps, so they either committed suicide or eventually died, not only physically but emotionally.

The sixth principle is VICTORY. When you have persevered and have achieved your desired outcome, that is the result: VICTORY. However, to get to this point, you need to visualize the outcome you desire. You must reject all negative and contrary thoughts but instead continue to focus on those thoughts that will bring life and not death.

In my father's situation, he refused to accept the thought of death because he was still young and wanted to live so he can accomplish what he felt he was called to do. Even though at times, the thoughts of death plagued him, he did not continue to entertain those thoughts for a long period of time. Instead, he kept speaking to himself, I want to live, I must live, I will live. He had to encourage himself with this self-talk because all around him there was death, destruction, and hopelessness. Even his friends, Pawel and Victor were giving up and spoke words of defeat and surrender. However, my father refused to accept their words of discouragement and even despite the harsh reality that surrounded them, he continued to focus on thoughts of victory and life. If you focus on defeat in your thought life, eventually what comes out of your mouth will be words of defeat. However, the opposite is also true. You can have what you say. If you continue to think about overcoming, the words that will come out of your mouth will be words of victory.

Granted this is not always easy to do, especially when death is lurking behind every corner and in one second your fate will be determined–life or death. So it takes a great amount of resolve to speak the opposite of what you are experiencing and believing for a good outcome. If you continue to speak to yourself this way, day after day, week after week, month after month and year after year you will experience your desired outcome which will culminate in VICTORY.

I believe my father spoke this way continually to himself during the years he spent at the concentration camps, after his escape and then his wanderings in the forest. His spirit was strong because he knew his purpose in life and many times he would ignore what was going on in his body physically. All the years in the camps had taken its toll on his body and a grown man weighing only 80 pounds must have suffered extreme pangs of hunger. Yet despite all this, his spirit dominated over the weakness of his body and he forced himself to go on to ultimately experience total victory.

The seventh principle is PROVIDENCE. We also must not dismiss the providence of God in our lives and in our circumstances. There are times in our lives when something out of the ordinary happens that can only be attributed as an act of God. We have all had experiences in our lives that defy explanation and leave us dumbfounded.

In my father's case, he had two such experiences that defy explanation. When he was arrested by the Gestapo and thrown into a prison cell, he was scheduled to be executed the following day. That same night he had a dream about a church with a cross on top of the steeple all lit up. To him, it symbolized a prophetic sign that he would not be executed and would be allowed to live. His interpretation of the dream turned out to be accurate. They did not execute him but instead sent him to a concentration camp in Ukraine.

Another example that defies explanation is when he came to a town after leaving the forest, two huge dogs rushed towards him and were about to attack him. However, weak as he was, he lifted a stick and started swinging at the dogs. To his amazement, the dogs instead of attacking him just wagged their tails and ran in the opposite direction. There was an old German woman who witnessed this and by her expression, you could see she was amazed by the way the two dogs had responded.

I am sure many survivors of concentration camps have had experiences where they were on the verge of death and suddenly there was divine intervention that caused their lives to be spared at the last minute. There comes a time in every person's life when they must rely on the God of Providence to help them overcome difficult and adverse situations.

My father at that time was not a religious man and he had to rely on his wits to help him survive the horrors of war. Yet, somehow during his suffering and imprisonment, there seemed to be a redemptive pattern that defined his experiences. Why was he not sent to Dora, which was one of the worst underground tunnel factories imaginable and many referred to it as a descent into hell? Most of his friends were transferred to Dora after the quarantine period in the little camp in Buchenwald. He was transferred to Julius Schönebeck and then Rottleberode where conditions were also terrible, but the prisoners did not die in such large numbers as they did in Dora. Also, he escaped death by jumping from the boxcar and running into the forest, whereas most of his friends from Rottleberode who were on the same transport, were burned to death in the barn at Gardelegen. Why was Pawel shot by the German soldiers when they were hiding in the forest and he escaped undetected?

It is difficult to find an answer to these questions, but I believe it was the providence of God that protected him. Towards the end of his life, my father developed a strong faith in God and attributed his survival to the providence of God.

Acknowledgments

I would like to acknowledge, Mrs. Stein of the Buchenwald Memorial, who is the head of the Memorial Archives. She was able to research and obtain documents on my father's incarceration at the camps in Buchenwald, Schönebeck and Rottleberode. I am very grateful to her since many of the documents in this book are the result of her efforts to locate them.

I would also like to acknowledge Lisa Schank, the educational colleague at the Buchenwald and Mittlebau-Dora Memorials Foundation. She helped Mrs. Stein but also spoke English so could explain what was written in the documents since it was in German.

I would also like to thank Gary Praeger who was my holocaust instructor at Rollins College at the Senior Center. He was very knowledgeable about the Holocaust and gifted me with a book called, "The History of the Dora Camp," by Andre Sellier which was very helpful in my research.

I would also like to thank my friend Pam Spinosi, who herself is a writer and who helped to encourage me in my writing. She also edited a few pages of the book and gave me some materials on writing a memoir.

I would also like to thank my friend, Gabriella Marcum who encouraged me and prayed for me to finish the book so that it could get out into the marketplace and be an inspiration to those who read it.

I would also like to thank Benny Smith who has prayed for close to a year to see this book become a reality.

I would also like to thank Pia Hansen, who is a teacher at the Lise Meitner School in Paderborn, Germany. She contacted the Archives Dept. at Buchenwald ahead of time and gave them the information about my father. I did not speak German so she was able to communicate with them and was kind enough to pick us up at the train station in Nordhausen to take us to the Dora tunnels and then drove us to Buchenwald.

I would also like to thank my long-time friend, Monica Nagy, who has been in the publishing industry for many years. She helped to design the book cover and advised me on matters related to the book.

I would also like to thank my family and especially, my husband who was very patient and assumed some of the household responsibilities while I focused on writing this book.

About the Authors

OXANA was born in New York, New York the same year her father immigrated to the United States. He brought her up to respect her heritage and sent her weekly from an early age to learn Ukrainian history and culture. This knowledge has served her well since she was able to work as an interpreter in the '90s for various organizations in the Ukraine and Israel. She has a BA from Queens College and a Master's in Religious Education from Gordon-Conwell Theological Seminary. After graduating, she worked in full-time ministry for a season in New York. She has also worked as a teacher and administrator and in various sales positions in the insurance industry. She resides in Florida with her husband of 23 years, Nicolas, who shares her heritage.

VALENTYN was born in Ukraine and grew up under the oppressive policies of the Communist regime. Against this backdrop Valentyn became a freedom-fighter and used the power of the pen to express his anti-Communist views. However, when the Nazis took over he found himself fighting against two fronts. He established himself as one of the leaders of the Ukrainian underground nationalist movement. After being arrested and surviving the holocaust, he immigrated to America in 1950 and continued his work. He became the editor of a publication called *Mission of Ukraine*, which was a division of the Association for the Liberation of Ukraine and was also active in a group called Americans to Free Captive Nations. His passion for freedom never abated even until his death in 1989.